AF410648

Dedication

This book is dedicated to Almighty Maa Samaleswari.

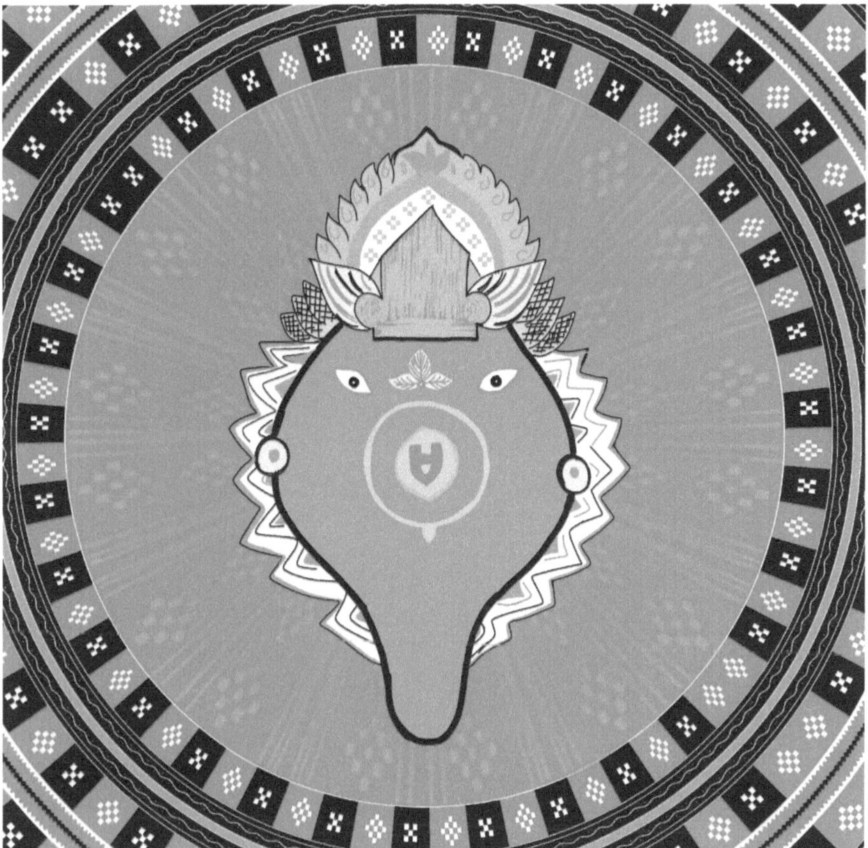

Maa Samaleswari

5E LESSON PLANS IN EDUCATION WITH METACOGNITIVE INTERVENTIONS

A HANDBOOK FOR TEACHERS

DR. VENKATESWAR MEHER & DR. RAJASHREE BARAL

Copyright © Dr. Venkateswar Meher & Dr. Rajashree Baral
All Rights Reserved.

This book has been published with all efforts taken to make the material error-free after the consent of the author. However, the author and the publisher do not assume and hereby disclaim any liability to any party for any loss, damage, or disruption caused by errors or omissions, whether such errors or omissions result from negligence, accident, or any other cause.

While every effort has been made to avoid any mistake or omission, this publication is being sold on the condition and understanding that neither the author nor the publishers or printers would be liable in any manner to any person by reason of any mistake or omission in this publication or for any action taken or omitted to be taken or advice rendered or accepted on the basis of this work. For any defect in printing or binding the publishers will be liable only to replace the defective copy by another copy of this work then available.

Contents

5E Lesson Plans in Education with Metacognitive Interventions
(A Handbook for Teachers)
First Edition

Written By
Dr. Venkateswar Meher
Dr. Rajashree Baral

Notion Press Publishing, Chandra Bhavan, Neheru Place, New Delhi-110019, India

Foreword

After reviewing the book, I can say that this book is a clear, concise, and well-written. It can be said that starting from Lesson Plan-1 to Lesson Plan-17 is relevant and theory based with some activities. Sufficient information about the activities is presented for readers to follow and explaining the rationale and procedures. The methods and approaches are generally appropriate. Proper clarification of a few details of methodology and provision of a rationale for the use of this particular method have also been mentioned in the preliminary pages.

The authors make a systematic contribution to the research literature in the area of Lesson Plans in Education. The conceptualization and the longitudinal nature of the work is a welcome addition. Overall, this is a high-quality manuscript that has implications for the theoretical basis, development, and maintenance of Lesson Plans in education. I must congratulate the authors for contributing such a great academic work in the field of education.

Best Wishes.

Dr. MPUANGNAN KOFI NKONKONYA, DEPARTMENT OF EDUCATION, MAMPONG TECHNICAL COLLEGE OF EDUCATION, GHANA

Preface

The book is based on 5E lesson plan with metacognitive interventions, which were developed based on the 'Education' syllabus of Council of Higher Secondary Education, Odisha, India.

Metacognition is the ability of individuals to apply previously acquired knowledge and experience to operate learning-related activities. This book is a part of Ph.D. thesis of Venkateswar Meher entitled "Impact of Metacognitive Interventions on Metacognitive Awareness, Self-Efficacy and Academic Achievement of Higher Secondary School Students". In the study, four metacognitive interventions were taken into consideration after intensive review of literature i.e., thinking aloud, brainstorming, concept mapping and self-assessment. The metacognitive interventions are multidimensional and interdisciplinary, which can be implemented in different subject areas of science and social science to make the teaching-learning process effective.

Development of students' metacognitive perspective is an important element in the constructivist approach of teaching in the classroom. In the process of constructing knowledge, both the teacher and students play active roles and they also evaluate the knowledge of their own, as a result, metacognition is also playing an important role in their learning as it refers to the awareness, understanding, and regulation of the teachers' and students' own cognitive functioning. Metacognition is the composition of knowledge of cognition and regulation of cognition, it can be said that metacognition is closely related to self-regulation, which is one of the crucial elements of constructivism. The metacognitive students are considered an integral part of the constructivist classroom, where they get the opportunity to interpret their viewpoints in a social setting, and become able to monitor and regulate their learning progress.

Keeping the relationship between metacognition and constructivism in mind, 5E lesson plans were developed, and in each step of the lesson plan, the metacognitive intervention was included. The constructivist 5E lesson plans consisted of five steps viz. engage, explore, explain, elaborate, and evaluate, where the students got opportunity for knowledge construction about the concepts of the subject matter. Keeping these five steps in mind, specific learning activities were planned to implement in the classroom. In each learning activity, the students were exposed to ask some sort of metacognitive questions to themselves. Apart from this, in each stage, specific metacognitive interventions were used to enable the students for understanding their own cognitive functions. In the Engage stage, the students were encouraged for thinking aloud, in Explore stage, the students were encouraged for brainstorming approach, in Explain stage, the students were encouraged for concept mapping strategy, in the Elaborate stage, the students were encouraged for both brainstorming and thinking aloud strategy, and in Evaluate stage, the students were encouraged for thinking aloud and self-assessment strategy.

For the experimentation purpose two groups were formed i.e., experimental and control group. For the students of experimental group 5E lesson plans were developed and suggestions from subject experts were taken for establishing content validity of the lesson plans before actual implementation. The lesson plans of the experimental group included metacognitive interventions like thinking aloud, concept mapping, brainstorming, and self-assessment. It also included some sorts of metacognitive questions and specific classroom activities in the classroom. The students of control group were taught following traditional approach. The experimentation was conducted in higher secondary schools for more than two months. The 5E lesson plan with metacognitive interventions were found to be effective in terms of self-efficacy, metacognitive awareness and academic achievement of higher secondary school students in education.

This book is beneficial for teachers for planning their lessons based on 5E lesson plan with metacognitive interventions.

Dr. Venkateswar Meher
Dr. Rajashree Baral

Acknowledgements

First and foremost, we bow in reverence before the Supreme God, the Almighty for the wonderful blessings bestowed on us abundantly during this research endeavour. At each and every moment of our life's journey we have experienced His loving presence enormously. We are grateful to you God, the Almighty.

It is indeed an honour for us to express our sincere gratitude from the bottom of my heart to my esteemed Prof. S. C. Panigrahi, Prof. Dayanand Sansanwal, Prof. Ramakanta Mohalik, Dr. Minaketana Pathy, Dr Annapurna Prusty, Dr Iswar Patel, Dr. Ashok Dansana, Dr Ramesh Ku. Parua, Dr Garudhwaja Barik, Kobid Padhan, Saptasagar Padhan, and Dr. Kofi whose continuous guidance, support, patience and encouragement motivated us from the very conception of idea of the research in the field and this enabled us to develop an understanding of the subject and to complete the book. Respected teachers you have nurtured us with research discipline all along our journey with you. Your insightful comments, constructivist ideas and criticisms at different stages of the research work were really thought provoking and helped us to focus on the development of the lesson plans. It was indeed a great privilege and honour for us to work with your guidance. Therefore, we owe a great deal to you for being such a wonderful mentor with integral humanism. We are really very much thankful to you for everything that you did for us in finalizing this research successfully.

From the bottom of my heart, we pay my heartiest thank to University Grant Commission, New Delhi for providing Junior Research Fellowship (JRF) throughout the research work, without this it would never been successful in our part.

From the core of our heart, we pay my heartfelt thanks to the principal of Hirakud Higher Secondary School, Hirakud (Sambalpur, Odisha) and principal of Burla NAC Higher Secondary School (Sambalpur, Odisha) for giving permission for conducting experimentation on this lesson plans. I am also thankful to the teaching staff of Education department of Hirakud Higher Secondary School and Burla NAC Higher Secondary School for their cooperation and assistance during the experimentation. I am equally thankful to the students of the selected higher secondary schools who participated throughout the study and cooperated for the experimentation. I am thankful to all the teaching and non-teaching staff of the school for their cooperation during the experimentation and data collection.

We thank Gangadhar Meher University, Amruta Vihar, Sambalpur for providing us opportunity to initiate and complete this research work successfully. Last but not the least, we are thankful to Notion Press Publisher, New Delhi for their efforts in publishing the book.

Dr. Venkateswar Meher
Dr. Rajashree Baral

CHAPTER ONE

LIFE PHILOSOPHY OF GANDHIJI

Lesson Plan-1

School: Higher Secondary School

Class: XII

Subject: Education

Topic: Life Philosophy of Gandhiji

Duration: 1 hour

TLM Required: Education textbook, Laptop to show pictures & Questions

Approach: Constructivist with Metacognitive Interventions

Phases: Engage, Explore, Explain, Elaborate, & Evaluate

Aim and Objective: The objective of this class is to make the students familiar about life philosophy of Mahatma Gandhi.

Learning Outcomes: After the class, the students will be able to

- understand the life philosophy of Gandhiji
- comprehend implications of life philosophy of Gandhiji
- demonstrate their knowledge in terms of life philosophy of Gandhiji

Engage:

In the first step of teaching i.e., Engage, the teacher favoured certain activities to capture and stimulate the attention, interest, thinking of the students. Here, the teacher tried to draw the child's curiosity towards learning and keep them mentally engaged in concepts, processes, or skills. So, keeping all these things in mind, the teacher performed the following activity.

Activity-1

The teacher showed some photographs of famous freedom fighters of India and their activities for the independence of the country, and asked them to share their reflections about the pictures with reference to education. Teacher: *Students, today, we shall make a discussion about* life philosophy of Gandhiji. *What do you know about Gandhiji? What does the life philosophy of Gandhiji include? What does the life philosophy of Gandhiji imply?* The teacher allowed each student to answer individually. During this process, the students were instructed to ask the following questions to themselves independently and note down their reflections in their notebook.

Q1. What do I know about this?

Q2. What do I do not know about this?

Q3. What kind of question is this?

Q4. What do I need to know about these questions?

Q5. What should I do to get an idea to answer these questions?

Q6. What kind of goal should I set for this?

Q7. How can I solve the problem?

Q8. Which strategy will help to find a solution to the problem?

Here, the students were encouraged to think-aloud about the questions asked to them. During the whole process, the think-aloud strategy was followed, and the responses of each student were recorded.

Explore:

In the second step of teaching, the teacher provided scope to the students to get involved with the topic and build up their own understanding in groups depending upon the feasibility. In this phase, the students in groups got an opportunity to develop current concepts, processes, and skills as they explored the learning environment. Here, the teacher manipulated learning materials related to the topic and asked the students to go through the same thoroughly in their group. In this step, the students got time to think, plan, investigate, and organize the information collected or received by them. The role of the teacher was as a facilitator.

Activity-2

After few minutes, the teacher divided the whole class into some small groups by assigning 5-6 students in each group. During this, the teacher allowed each student of each group to present a solution to the problem. In this stage, each student was encouraged to ask the necessary questions to other students of their groups. So, each student presented solutions to the problem before the group representative and they arrived at the consensus. After this, the group discussed their procedures to give solutions to the problem, where each member presented his/her procedures before others, and others listened to the presentation, analysed critically, and asked critical questions. At the end of the presentation, the students arrived at the consensus about the procedures of solving the problems. In this stage, the students were encouraged to ask the following questions to themselves individually.

Q1. How did I get my answer?

Q2. What will be other possible solutions to these problems?

Q3. Which strategy is the best to solve this problem?

Q4. How did I arrange the information for solving the problems?

Q5. What kinds of difficulties did you face to solve these problems?

Q6. How did I think about the procedures?

Q7. What are the limitations of this strategy?

During this stage, the students were encouraged to think aloud for finding possible solutions to the problem and work collaboratively. In this stage, the brainstorming method was encouraged.

Explain:

In the third step of teaching, the teacher provided the opportunity to the students for assimilation, where the students tried to connect their previous knowledge with the current learning for the conceptual clarity. Here, more focus was on students' attention on a specific part of engagement and exploration, which helped students to verbalize their conceptual understanding or demonstrating skills.

Activity-3

In this phase, the teacher encouraged the use of concept mapping. Each group representative discussed with their members of the group and presented the answers to the given problem before the group and showed a concept map for better visualisation and understanding. The group representatives got equal time to demonstrate their procedure of solving the problem, and the others actively listened to the presenters and posed essential questions to themselves.

Q1. How is this the solution to the problems?

Q2. Are there any other possible solutions?

Q3. Am I able to understand this solution?

Q4. What was running in my mind while listening to the solutions?

Q5. How is my procedure different from others?

During this phase, the teacher also got the opportunity to introduce the definition of the concepts, skills, process, and behaviour. Here, the teacher encouraged the use of concept mapping strategy among students and assisted them to relate a concept with other sub-concepts in diagrams. The rationale behind the use of concept mapping strategy was to help the students in understanding relationship between concept and sub-concepts relating to the topic. Here the students worked in group to create concept maps related to the topic and showed to each other.

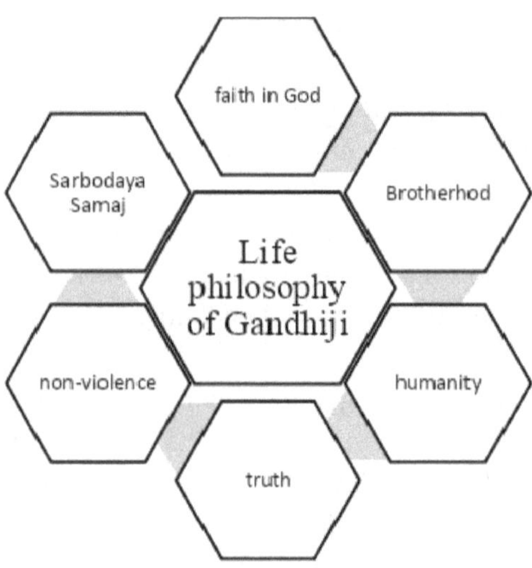

Figure-1: Life philosophy of Gandhiji

The teacher observed the whole process and provided the required assistance wherever required for a better understanding of the students. At the end of this phase, the teacher helped the group to arrive at the consensus of the problem.

Elaborate:

In the fourth step, the focus was given to students' conceptual understanding to allow them for practising different skills and behaviour. Here, the opportunity was provided to the students to apply or extend the previously learned concepts and experiences to the new situations, as a result of which, the students developed better understanding, generated more information, and learned adequate skills. Here, the teacher helped the students to apply their learned knowledge and develop a deeper understanding of the subject matter.

Activity: 4

The teacher gave a question card to the students comprising of analysis-based questions related to the topic and asked them to discuss the possible answers. Here, the teacher brought the attention of the students in front of the class and provided an opportunity to each group representative to present the answers by summarizing the responses of each member of the group. The other students were encouraged to pose essential questions before the group representative. Here, the teacher provided a question card to each group for discussion.

Question Card

Q1. Gandhiji was a philosopher and seeker after truth. Elucidate.

Q2. What are the implications of life philosophy of Gandhiji in 21st century?

Q3. Analyse the key features concerning to life philosophy of Gandhiji and prepare a concept map.

During the whole process, the students were encouraged to think aloud about the questions presented to them and asked them the following questions to themselves.

Q1. How are these questions related to the previous questions?

Q2. How will I use previous information to solve these questions?

Q3. Will I be able to connect my previous knowledge to this problem?

Q4. What kinds of difficulties am I facing to associate previous information?

Q5. What kinds of thoughts are running inside my mind concerned with this problem?

Q6. How can I solve these problems?

The students presented their answers in the group before the group representative, and the representative noted down the responses of each member and summarized the same. Finally, the representative presented the answers before others. The teacher encouraged other students to ask their queries to the representative. In this stage, both thinking-aloud and concept mapping strategies were used.

Evaluate:

In the fifth step i.e., Evaluate, the teacher and students both determined the extent to which the learning and understanding have taken place about the topic, i.e., Life Philosophy of Gandhiji. Here, students were provided an opportunity to review and assess their learning in a summative form. Here, the students were encouraged to assess their understanding, abilities, skills, and behaviour related to the topic. The teacher gave due emphasis on reflection by following both formal and informal assessment procedures rather than traditional quizzes. The teacher gave due importance to self-assessment and writing assignments. The teacher preferred the self-assessment technique in this step, where the students got the opportunity to evaluate their own academic works and learning progress. Through self-assessment, the students got opportunity to identify the gap in their knowledge, track their own progress, set goals, and revise their works.

Activity-5

The teacher favoured some sorts of reflective questions related to the topic before the students and their responses were gathered orally. The reason behind the use of reflective questions was to encourage students for reflecting on their learning skills and generating relevant questions and ideas for propelling future learning experiences. In this stage, the teacher encouraged the students to ask questions about themselves related to their learning activities, processes, and behaviour.

Q1. Did I understand what I need to understand?

Q2. In which condition I learned the most?

Q3. Where did I feel difficulty in understanding the topic?

Q4. How did I learn the subject matter?

Q5. How my learning style is different from others?

Q6. Did I plan properly to adopt procedures for finding the solution to the problems?

Q7. Did I able to learn correctly about life philosophy of Gandhiji?

Q8. How did I learn the topic?

Q9. Do I keep in mind the way of my learning? How?

Q10. Am I satisfied with my learning style?

Q11. What is the lacuna in my learning?

Q12. How can I learn better?

The teacher gathered and analysed the responses of the students and measured the learning outcomes of the lesson. The teacher focused on students' abilities to formulate their own meaning and definitions about the topic. Here, the teacher used self-assessment techniques through this phase.

Homework

At the end of the class, the teachers provided some home works related to the topic discussed before the class. The home works were given based on the students' learning and experience on the life philosophy of Gandhiji and also, they were instructed to gather information about educational philosophy of Gandhiji, which was to be discussed in the next class. So, in this field, the teacher tried to prepare the students independently for the next class considering it as a technique of students' inspiration for further learning activities.

'The core points'- The students developed their understanding regarding the life philosophy of Gandhiji and constructed new knowledge.

CHAPTER TWO

EDUCATIONAL PHILOSOPHY OF GANDHIJI-I

Lesson Plan-2

School: Higher Secondary School

Class: XII

Subject: Education

Topic: Educational Philosophy of Gandhiji-I

Duration: 1 hour

TLM Required: Education textbook, Laptop to show pictures, & Question

Approach: Constructivist with Metacognitive Interventions

Phases: Engage, Explore, Explain, Elaborate, & Evaluate

Aim and Objective: The objective of this class is to develop understanding among students about educational philosophy of Mahatma Gandhi.

Learning Outcomes: After the class, the students will be able to

- understand Gandhiji's view on concept of education
- comprehend aims of education and curriculum as prescribed by Gandhiji
- demonstrate their knowledge in terms of educational philosophy of Gandhiji

Engage:

In the first step of teaching i.e., Engage, the teacher favoured certain activities to capture and stimulate the attention, interest, thinking of the

students. Here, the teacher tried to draw the child's curiosity towards learning and keep them mentally engaged in concepts, processes, or skills. So, keeping all these things in mind, the teacher performed the following activity.

Activity-1

The teacher showed some photographs of great Indian and western philosophers like Gandhiji, Tagore, Vivekananda, Plato, Pestalozzi, John Dewey, and asked them to share their ideas about their educational contributions. Teacher: *Students, today, we shall make a discussion about educational philosophy of Gandhiji. What does the educational philosophy of Gandhiji include? How does Gandhiji define education and prescribe aims of education?* The teacher allowed each student to answer individually. During this process, the students were instructed to ask the following questions to themselves independently and note down their reflections in their notebook.

Q1. What do I know about this?

Q2. What do I do not know about this?

Q3. What kind of question is this?

Q4. What do I need to know about these questions?

Q5. What should I do to get an idea to answer these questions?

Q6. What kind of goal should I set for this?

Q7. How can I solve the problem?

Q8. Which strategy will help to find a solution to the problem?

Here, the students were encouraged to think-aloud about the questions asked to them. During the whole process, the think-aloud strategy was followed, and the responses of each student were recorded.

Explore:

In the second step of teaching, the teacher provided scope to the students to get involved with the topic and build up their own understanding in groups depending upon the feasibility. In this phase, the students in groups got an opportunity to develop current concepts, processes, and skills as they explored the learning environment. Here, the teacher manipulated learning materials related to the topic and asked the students to go through the same thoroughly in their group. In this step, the students got time to think, plan, investigate, and organize the information collected or received by them. The role of the teacher was as a facilitator.

Activity-2

After few minutes, the teacher divided the whole class into some small groups by assigning 5-6 students in each group. During this, the teacher allowed each student of each group to present a solution to the problem. In this stage, each student was encouraged to ask the necessary questions to other students of their groups. So, each student presented solutions to the problem before the group representative and they arrived at the consensus. After this, the group discussed their procedures to give solutions to the problem, where each member presented his/her procedures before others, and others listened to the presentation, analysed critically, and asked critical questions. At the end of the presentation, the students arrived at the consensus about the procedures of solving the problems. In this stage, the students were encouraged to ask the following questions to themselves individually.

Q1. How did I get my answer?

Q2. What will be other possible solutions to these problems?

Q3. Which strategy is the best to solve this problem?

Q4. How did I arrange the information for solving the problems?

Q5. What kinds of difficulties did you face to solve these problems?

Q6. How did I think about the procedures?

Q7. What are the limitations of this strategy?

During this stage, the students were encouraged to think aloud for finding possible solutions to the problem and work collaboratively. In this stage, the brainstorming method was encouraged.

Explain:

In the third step of teaching, the teacher provided the opportunity to the students for assimilation, where the students tried to connect their previous knowledge with the current learning for the conceptual clarity. Here, more focus was on students' attention on a specific part of engagement and exploration, which helped students to verbalize their conceptual understanding or demonstrating skills.

Activity-3

In this phase, the group representative presented the answers to the given problem before the group and showed a concept map for better visualisation and understanding. The group representatives got equal time to demonstrate their procedure of solving the problem, and the others actively listened to the presenters and posed essential questions to themselves.

Q1. How is this the solution to the problems?

Q2. Are there any other possible solutions?

Q3. Am I able to understand this solution?

Q4. What was running in my mind while listening to the solutions?

Q5. How is my procedure different from others?

During this phase, the teacher also got the opportunity to introduce the definition of the concepts, skills, process, and behaviour. Here, the teacher encouraged the use of concept mapping strategy among students and assisted them to relate a concept with other sub-concepts in diagrams. The rationale behind the use of concept mapping strategy was to help the students in understanding relationship between concept and sub-concepts relating to the topic. Here the students worked in group to create concept maps related to the topic and showed to each other.

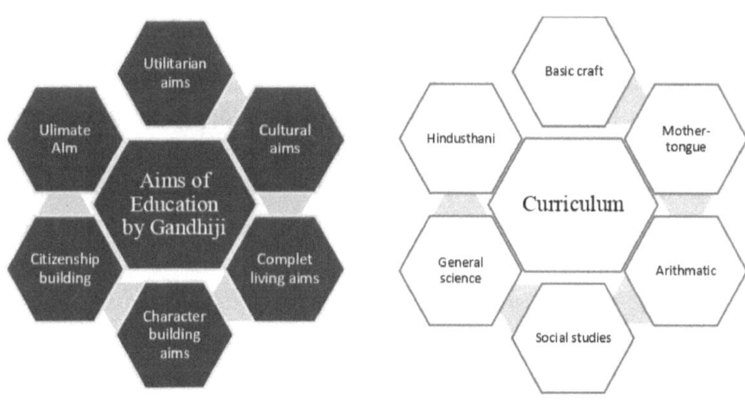

Figure-2: Aims of education & curriculum accoridng to Gandhiji

The teacher observed the whole process and provided the required assistance wherever required for a better understanding of the students. At the end of this phase, the teacher helped the group to arrive at the consensus of the problem.

Elaborate:

In the fourth step, the focus was given to students' conceptual understanding to allow them for practising different skills and behaviour. Here, the opportunity was provided to the students to apply or extend the previously learned concepts and experiences to the new situations, as

a result of which, the students developed better understanding, generated more information, and learned adequate skills. Here, the teacher helped the students to apply their learned knowledge and develop a deeper understanding of the subject matter.

Activity: 4

The teacher gave a question card to the students comprising of analysis-based questions related to the topic and asked them to discuss the possible answers. Here, the teacher brought the attention of the students in front of the class and provided an opportunity to each group representative to present the answers by summarizing the responses of each member of the group. The other students were encouraged to pose essential questions before the group representative. Here, the teacher provided a question card to each group for discussion.

Question Card

Q1. Analyse the relevance of aims of education prescribed by Gandhiji in present era.

Q2. What is the relevance of curriculum prescribed by Gandhiji?

Q3. Analyse the educational philosophy of Gandhiji in terms of concept of education, aims of education and curriculum and represent in concept maps?

During the whole process, the students were encouraged to think aloud about the questions presented to them and asked them the following questions to themselves.

Q1. How are these questions related to the previous questions?

Q2. How will I use previous information to solve these questions?

Q3. Will I be able to connect my previous knowledge to this problem?

Q4. What kinds of difficulties am I facing to associate previous information?

Q5. What kinds of thoughts are running inside my mind concerned with this problem?

Q6. How can I solve these problems?

The students presented their answers in the group before the group representative, and the representative noted down the responses of each member and summarized the same. Finally, the representative presented the answers before others. The teacher encouraged other students to ask their queries to the representative. In this stage, both thinking-aloud and concept mapping strategies were used.

Evaluate:

In the fifth step i.e., Evaluate, the teacher and students both determined the extent to which the learning and understanding have taken place about

the topic, i.e., educational philosophy of Gandhiji-I. Here, students were provided an opportunity to review and assess their learning in a summative form. Here, the students were encouraged to assess their understanding, abilities, skills, and behaviour related to the topic. The teacher gave due emphasis on reflection by following both formal and informal assessment procedures rather than traditional quizzes. The teacher gave due importance to self-assessment and writing assignments. The teacher preferred the self-assessment technique in this step, where the students got the opportunity to evaluate their own academic works and learning progress. Through self-assessment, the students got opportunity to identify the gap in their knowledge, track their own progress, set goals, and revise their works.

Activity-5

The teacher favoured some sorts of reflective questions related to the topic before the students and their responses were gathered orally. The reason behind the use of reflective questions was to encourage students for reflecting on their learning skills and generating relevant questions and ideas for propelling future learning experiences. In this stage, the teacher encouraged the students to ask questions about themselves related to their learning activities, processes, and behaviour.

Q1. Did I understand what I need to understand?

Q2. In which condition I learned the most?

Q3. Where did I feel difficulty in understanding the topic?

Q4. How did I learn the subject matter?

Q5. How my learning style is different from others?

Q6. Did I plan properly to adopt procedures for finding the solution to the problems?

Q7. Did I able to learn correctly about educational philosophy of Gandhiji-I?

Q8. How did I learn the topic?

Q9. Do I keep in mind the way of my learning? How?

Q10. Am I satisfied with my learning style?

Q11. What is the lacuna in my learning?

Q12. How can I learn better?

The teacher gathered and analysed the responses of the students and measured the learning outcomes of the lesson. The teacher focused on students' abilities to formulate their own meaning and definitions about the topic. Here, the teacher used self-assessment technique.

Homework

At the end of the class, the teachers provided some home works related to the topic discussed before the class. The home works were given based on the students' learning and experience on the educational philosophy of Gandhiji-I and also, they were instructed to gather more information about the educational philosophy of Gandhiji-I with reference to methods of teaching, role of teacher, and discipline, which was to be discussed in the next class. So, in this field, the teacher tried to prepare the students independently for the next class considering it as a technique of students' inspiration for further learning activities.

'The core points'- The students developed their understanding regarding the educational philosophy of Gandhiji and constructed new knowledge.

CHAPTER THREE

Educational Philosophy of Gandhiji-II

Lesson Plan-3

School: Higher Secondary School

Class: XII

Subject: Education

Topic: Educational Philosophy of Gandhiji-II

Duration: 1 hour

TLM Required: Education textbook, Laptop to show pictures, & Question

Approach: Constructivist with Metacognitive Interventions

Phases: Engage, Explore, Explain, Elaborate, & Evaluate

Aim and Objective: The objective of this class is to develop deeper understanding among students about educational philosophy of Mahatma Gandhi.

Learning Outcomes: After the class, the students will be able to

- understand Gandhiji's view on methods of teaching
- comprehend place of teacher and discipline as prescribed by Gandhiji
- demonstrate their knowledge in terms of educational philosophy of Gandhiji

Engage:

In the first step of teaching i.e., Engage, the teacher favoured certain activities to capture and stimulate the attention, interest, thinking of the

students. Here, the teacher tried to draw the child's curiosity towards learning and keep them mentally engaged in concepts, processes, or skills. So, keeping all these things in mind, the teacher performed the following activity.

Activity-1

The teacher asked some questions related to the life philosophy of Gandhiji and asked them to give their view points on aims of education and curriculum as prescribed by Gandhiji. Teacher: *Students, today, we shall make a discussion about educational philosophy of Gandhiji. What is the view of Gandhiji on place of teacher and discipline of students? What is the educational thought of Gandhiji on textbook, religious education and women's education?* The teacher allowed each student to answer individually. During this process, the students were instructed to ask the following questions to themselves independently and note down their reflections in their notebook.

Q1. What do I know about this?

Q2. What do I do not know about this?

Q3. What kind of question is this?

Q4. What do I need to know about these questions?

Q5. What should I do to get an idea to answer these questions?

Q6. What kind of goal should I set for this?

Q7. How can I solve the problem?

Q8. Which strategy will help to find a solution to the problem?

Here, the students were encouraged to think-aloud about the questions asked to them. During the whole process, the thinking-aloud strategy was followed, and the responses of each student were recorded.

Explore:

In the second step of teaching, the teacher provided scope to the students to get involved with the topic and build up their own understanding in groups depending upon the feasibility. In this phase, the students in groups got an opportunity to develop current concepts, processes, and skills as they explored the learning environment. Here, the teacher manipulated learning materials related to the topic and asked the students to go through the same thoroughly in their group. In this step, the students got time to think, plan, investigate, and organize the information collected or received by them. The role of the teacher was as a facilitator.

Activity-2

After few minutes, the teacher divided the whole class into some small groups by assigning 5-6 students in each group. During this, the teacher allowed each student of each group to present a solution to the problem. In this stage, each student was encouraged to ask the necessary questions to other students of their groups. So, each student presented solutions to the problem before the group representative and they arrived at the consensus. After this, the group discussed their procedures to give solutions to the problem, where each member presented his/her procedures before others, and others listened to the presentation, analysed critically, and asked critical questions. At the end of the presentation, the students arrived at the consensus about the procedures of solving the problems. In this stage, the students were encouraged to ask the following questions to themselves individually.

Q1. How did I get my answer?

Q2. What will be other possible solutions to these problems?

Q3. Which strategy is the best to solve this problem?

Q4. How did I arrange the information for solving the problems?

Q5. What kinds of difficulties did you face to solve these problems?

Q6. How did I think about the procedures?

Q7. What are the limitations of this strategy?

During this stage, the students were encouraged to think aloud for finding possible solutions to the problem and work collaboratively. In this stage, the brainstorming method was encouraged.

Explain:

In the third step of teaching, the teacher provided the opportunity to the students for assimilation, where the students tried to connect their previous knowledge with the current learning for the conceptual clarity. Here, more focus was on students' attention on a specific part of engagement and exploration, which helped students to verbalize their conceptual understanding or demonstrating skills.

Activity-3

In this phase, the group representative presented the answers to the given problem before the group and showed a concept map for better visualisation and understanding. The group representatives got equal time to demonstrate their procedure of solving the problem, and the others actively listened to the presenters and posed essential questions to themselves.

Q1. How is this the solution to the problems?

Q2. Are there any other possible solutions?

Q3. Am I able to understand this solution?

Q4. What was running in my mind while listening to the solutions?

Q5. How is my procedure different from others?

During this phase, the teacher also got the opportunity to introduce the definition of the concepts, skills, process, and behaviour. Here, the teacher encouraged the use of concept mapping strategy among students and assisted them to relate a concept with other sub-concepts in diagrams. The rationale behind the use of concept mapping strategy was to help the students in understanding relationship between concept and sub-concepts relating to the topic. Here the students worked in group to create concept maps related to the topic and showed to each other.

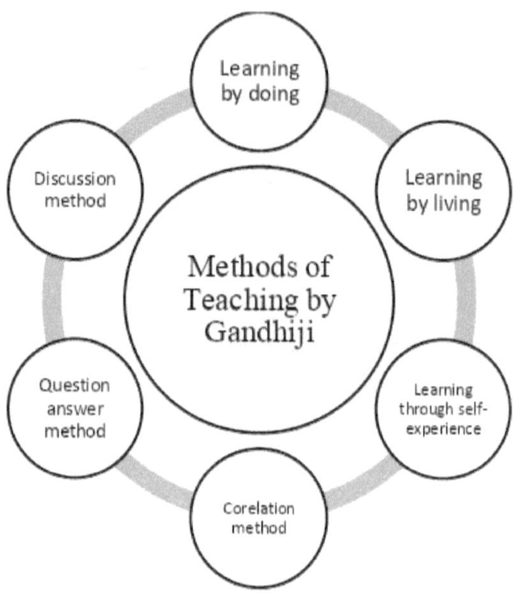

Figure-3: Methods of teaching according to Gandhiji

The teacher observed the whole process and provided the required assistance wherever required for a better understanding of the students. At the end of this phase, the teacher helped the group to arrive at the consensus of the problem.

Elaborate:

In the fourth step, the focus was given to students' conceptual understanding to allow them for practising different skills and behaviour. Here, the opportunity was provided to the students to apply or extend the previously learned concepts and experiences to the new situations, as a result of which, the students developed better understanding, generated more information, and learned adequate skills. Here, the teacher helped the students to apply their learned knowledge and develop a deeper understanding of the subject matter.

Activity: 4

The teacher gave a question card to the students comprising of analysis-based questions related to the topic and asked them to discuss the possible answers. Here, the teacher brought the attention of the students in front of the class and provided an opportunity to each group representative to present the answers by summarizing the responses of each member of the group. The other students were encouraged to pose essential questions before the group representative. Here, the teacher provided a question card to each group for discussion.

Question Card

Q1. Analyse the relevance of methods of teaching prescribed by Gandhiji in present era.

Q2. What is the relevance of women education prescribed by Gandhiji?

Q3. Analyse the educational philosophy of Gandhiji in terms of methods of teaching, place of teacher, discipline and represent your answers in concept maps?

During the whole process, the students were encouraged to think aloud about the questions presented to them and asked them the following questions to themselves.

Q1. How are these questions related to the previous questions?

Q2. How will I use previous information to solve these questions?

Q3. Will I be able to connect my previous knowledge to this problem?

Q4. What kinds of difficulties am I facing to associate previous information?

Q5. What kinds of thoughts are running inside my mind concerned with this problem?

Q6. How can I solve these problems?

The students presented their answers in the group before the group representative, and the representative noted down the responses of each member and summarized the same. Finally, the representative presented the answers before others. The teacher encouraged other students to ask their queries to the representative. In this stage, both thinking-aloud and concept mapping strategies were used.

Evaluate:

In the fifth step i.e., Evaluate, the teacher and students both determined the extent to which the learning and understanding have taken place about the topic, i.e., educational philosophy of Gandhiji-II. Here, students were provided an opportunity to review and assess their learning in a summative form. Here, the students were encouraged to assess their understanding, abilities, skills, and behaviour related to the topic. The teacher gave due emphasis on reflection by following both formal and informal assessment procedures rather than traditional quizzes. The teacher gave due importance to self-assessment and writing assignments. The teacher preferred the self-assessment technique in this step, where the students got the opportunity to evaluate their own academic works and learning progress. Through self-assessment, the students got opportunity to identify the gap in their knowledge, track their own progress, set goals, and revise their works.

Activity-5

The teacher favoured some sorts of reflective questions related to the topic before the students and their responses were gathered orally. The reason behind the use of reflective questions was to encourage students for reflecting on their learning skills and generating relevant questions and ideas for propelling future learning experiences. In this stage, the teacher encouraged the students to ask questions about themselves related to their learning activities, processes, and behaviour.

Q1. Did I understand what I need to understand?

Q2. In which condition I learned the most?

Q3. Where did I feel difficulty in understanding the topic?

Q4. How did I learn the subject matter?

Q5. How my learning style is different from others?

Q6. Did I plan properly to adopt procedures for finding the solution to the problems?

Q7. Did I able to learn correctly about educational philosophy of Gandhiji-II?

Q8. How did I learn the topic?

Q9. Do I keep in mind the way of my learning? How?

Q10. Am I satisfied with my learning style?

Q11. What is the lacuna in my learning?

Q12. How can I learn better?

The teacher gathered and analysed the responses of the students and measured the learning outcomes of the lesson. The teacher focused on students' abilities to formulate their own meaning and definitions about the topic. Here, the teacher used self-assessment technique.

Homework

At the end of the class, the teachers provided some home works related to the topic discussed before the class. The home works were given based on the students' learning and experience on the educational philosophy of Gandhiji-I and also, they were instructed to gather information about basic education of Gandhij, which was to be discussed in the next class. So, in this field, the teacher tried to prepare the students independently for the next class considering it as a technique of students' inspiration for further learning activities.

'The core points'- The students developed their deeper understanding regarding the life philosophy of Gandhiji and constructed new knowledge.

CHAPTER FOUR

BASIC EDUCATION-I

Lesson Plan-4

School: Higher Secondary School

Class: XII

Subject: Education

Topic: Basic Education-I

Duration: 1 hour

TLM Required: Education textbook, Laptop to show pictures, & Question

Approach: Constructivist with Metacognitive Interventions

Phases: Engage, Explore, Explain, Elaborate, & Evaluate

Aim and Objective: The objective of this class is to develop understanding among students about rational of Gandhiji's basic education.

Learning Outcomes: After the class, the students will be able to

- understand the concept of basic education
- comprehend main features/principles of basic education
- demonstrate their knowledge in terms of basic education

Engage:

In the first step of teaching i.e., Engage, the teacher favoured certain activities to capture and stimulate the attention, interest, thinking of the students. Here, the teacher tried to draw the child's curiosity towards learning and keep them mentally engaged in concepts, processes, or skills. So, keeping all these things in mind, the teacher performed the following activity.

Activity-1

The teacher asked some questions related to the life philosophy of Gandhiji and asked them to give their view points on educational contributions of Gandhiji in Indian context. Teacher: *Students, today, we shall make a discussion about basic education of Gandhiji. What is meant by basic education? What are the key features of basic education?* The teacher allowed each student to answer individually. During this process, the students were instructed to ask the following questions to themselves independently and note down their reflections in their notebook.

Q1. What do I know about this?

Q2. What do I do not know about this?

Q3. What kind of question is this?

Q4. What do I need to know about these questions?

Q5. What should I do to get an idea to answer these questions?

Q6. What kind of goal should I set for this?

Q7. How can I solve the problem?

Q8. Which strategy will help to find a solution to the problem?

Here, the students were encouraged to think-aloud about the questions asked to them. During the whole process, the thinking-aloud strategy was followed, and the responses of each student were recorded.

Explore:

In the second step of teaching, the teacher provided scope to the students to get involved with the topic and build up their own understanding in groups depending upon the feasibility. In this phase, the students in groups got an opportunity to develop current concepts, processes, and skills as they explored the learning environment. Here, the teacher manipulated learning materials related to the topic and asked the students to go through the same thoroughly in their group. In this step, the students got time to think, plan, investigate, and organize the information collected or received by them. The role of the teacher was as a facilitator.

Activity-2

After few minutes, the teacher divided the whole class into some small groups by assigning 5-6 students in each group. During this, the teacher allowed each student of each group to present a solution to the problem. In this stage, each student was encouraged to ask the necessary questions to other students of their groups. So, each student presented solutions to the problem before the group representative and they arrived at the consensus. After this, the group discussed their procedures to give solutions to the problem, where each member presented his/her procedures before others, and others listened to the presentation, analysed critically, and asked critical questions. At the end of the presentation, the students arrived at the consensus about the procedures of solving the problems. In this stage, the students were encouraged to ask the following questions to themselves individually.

Q1. How did I get my answer?

Q2. What will be other possible solutions to these problems?

Q3. Which strategy is the best to solve this problem?

Q4. How did I arrange the information for solving the problems?

Q5. What kinds of difficulties did you face to solve these problems?

Q6. How did I think about the procedures?

Q7. What are the limitations of this strategy?

During this stage, the students were encouraged to think aloud for finding possible solutions to the problem and work collaboratively. In this stage, the brainstorming method was encouraged.

Explain:

In the third step of teaching, the teacher provided the opportunity to the students for assimilation, where the students tried to connect their previous knowledge with the current learning for the conceptual clarity. Here, more focus was on students' attention on a specific part of engagement and exploration, which helped students to verbalize their conceptual understanding or demonstrating skills.

Activity-3

In this phase, the group representative presented the answers to the given problem before the group and showed a concept map for better visualisation and understanding. The group representatives got equal time to demonstrate their procedure of solving the problem, and the others actively listened to the presenters and posed essential questions to themselves.

Q1. How is this the solution to the problems?

Q2. Are there any other possible solutions?

Q3. Am I able to understand this solution?

Q4. What was running in my mind while listening to the solutions?

Q5. How is my procedure different from others?

During this phase, the teacher also got the opportunity to introduce the definition of the concepts, skills, process, and behaviour. Here, the teacher encouraged the use of concept mapping strategy among students and assisted them to relate a concept with other sub-concepts in diagrams.

The rationale behind the use of concept mapping strategy was to help the students in understanding relationship between concept and sub-concepts relating to the topic. Here the students worked in group to create concept maps related to the topic and showed to each other.

Figure-4: Features of basic education

The teacher observed the whole process and provided the required assistance wherever required for a better understanding of the students. At the end of this phase, the teacher helped the group to arrive at the consensus of the problem.

Elaborate:

In the fourth step, the focus was given to students' conceptual understanding to allow them for practising different skills and behaviour. Here, the opportunity was provided to the students to apply or extend the previously learned concepts and experiences to the new situations, as a result of which, the students developed better understanding, generated more information, and learned adequate skills. Here, the teacher helped the students to apply their learned knowledge and develop a deeper understanding of the subject matter.

Activity: 4

The teacher gave a question card to the students comprising of analysis-based questions related to the topic and asked them to discuss the possible answers. Here, the teacher brought the attention of the students in front of the class and provided an opportunity to each group representative to present the answers by summarizing the responses of each member of the group. The other students were encouraged to pose essential questions before the group representative. Here, the teacher provided a question card to each group for discussion.

Question Card

Q1. Analyse the concept of basic education and define it in your own ways.

Q2. What is the relevance of the key features of basic education in present context?

Q3. Analyse the main principles of basic education in Indian context and represent your answers in concept maps?

During the whole process, the students were encouraged to think aloud about the questions presented to them and asked them the following questions to themselves.

Q1. How are these questions related to the previous questions?

Q2. How will I use previous information to solve these questions?

Q3. Will I be able to connect my previous knowledge to this problem?

Q4. What kinds of difficulties am I facing to associate previous information?

Q5. What kinds of thoughts are running inside my mind concerned with this problem?

Q6. How can I solve these problems?

The students presented their answers in the group before the group representative, and the representative noted down the responses of each member and summarized the same. Finally, the representative presented the answers before others. The teacher encouraged other students to ask their queries to the representative. In this stage, both thinking-aloud and concept mapping strategies were used.

Evaluate:

In the fifth step i.e., Evaluate, the teacher and students both determined the extent to which the learning and understanding have taken place about the topic, i.e., basic education-I. Here, students were provided an opportunity to review and assess their learning in a summative form. Here, the students were encouraged to assess their understanding, abilities, skills, and behaviour related to the topic. The teacher gave due emphasis on reflection by following both formal and informal assessment procedures rather than traditional quizzes. The teacher gave due importance to self-assessment and writing assignments. The teacher preferred the self-assessment technique in this step, where the students got the opportunity to evaluate their own academic works and learning progress. Through self-assessment, the students got opportunity to identify the gap in their knowledge, track their own progress, set goals, and revise their works.

Activity-5

The teacher favoured some sorts of reflective questions related to the topic before the students and their responses were gathered orally. The reason behind the use of reflective questions was to encourage students for reflecting on their learning skills and generating relevant questions and ideas for propelling future learning experiences. In this stage, the teacher encouraged the students to ask questions about themselves related to their learning activities, processes, and behaviour.

Q1. Did I understand what I need to understand?

Q2. In which condition I learned the most?

Q3. Where did I feel difficulty in understanding the topic?

Q4. How did I learn the subject matter?

Q5. How my learning style is different from others?

Q6. Did I plan properly to adopt procedures for finding the solution to the problems?

Q7. Did I able to learn correctly about basic education-I?

Q8. How did I learn the topic?

Q9. Do I keep in mind the way of my learning? How?

Q10. Am I satisfied with my learning style?

Q11. What is the lacuna in my learning?

Q12. How can I learn better?

The teacher gathered and analysed the responses of the students and measured the learning outcomes of the lesson. The teacher focused on students' abilities to formulate their own meaning and definitions about the topic. Here, the teacher used self-assessment technique.

Homework

At the end of the class, the teachers provided some home works related to the topic discussed before the class. The home works were given based on the students' learning and experience on basic education-I and also, they were instructed to gather information about basic education with reference to advantages and failure of basic education, which was to be discussed in the next class. So, in this field, the teacher tried to prepare the students independently for the next class considering it as a technique of students' inspiration for further learning activities.

'The core points'- The students developed their understanding regarding basic education of Gandhiji and constructed new knowledge.

CHAPTER FIVE

BASIC EDUCATION-II

Lesson Plan-5

School: Higher Secondary School

Class: XII

Subject: Education

Topic: Basic Education-II

Duration: 1 hour

TLM Required: Education textbook, Laptop to show pictures, & Question

Approach: Constructivist with Metacognitive Interventions

Phases: Engage, Explore, Explain, Elaborate, & Evaluate

Aim and Objective: The objective of this class is to develop deeper understanding among students about rational of Gandhiji's basic education.

Learning Outcomes: After the class, the students will be able to

- understand the advantages of basic education
- comprehend causes of failure of basic education
- demonstrate their knowledge in terms of basic education

Engage:

In the first step of teaching i.e., Engage, the teacher favoured certain activities to capture and stimulate the attention, interest, thinking of the students. Here, the teacher tried to draw the child's curiosity towards learning and keep them mentally engaged in concepts, processes, or skills. So, keeping all these things in mind, the teacher performed the following activity.

Activity-1

The teacher asked some questions related to the concept and main principles of basic education. The teacher also showed some pictures of manual works done by the people at rural areas and asked them to give their viewpoints basic education in Indian context. Teacher: *Students, today, we shall make a discussion about the advantages of basic education of Gandhiji. Why basic education is beneficial for the people? What are the factors responsible for the failure of basic education?* The teacher allowed each student to answer individually. During this process, the students were instructed to ask the following questions to themselves independently and note down their reflections in their notebook.

Q1. What do I know about this?

Q2. What do I do not know about this?

Q3. What kind of question is this?

Q4. What do I need to know about these questions?

Q5. What should I do to get an idea to answer these questions?

Q6. What kind of goal should I set for this?

Q7. How can I solve the problem?

Q8. Which strategy will help to find a solution to the problem?

Here, the students were encouraged to think-aloud about the questions asked to them. During the whole process, the thinking-aloud strategy was followed, and the responses of each student were recorded.

Explore:

In the second step of teaching, the teacher provided scope to the students to get involved with the topic and build up their own understanding in groups depending upon the feasibility. In this phase, the students in groups got an opportunity to develop current concepts, processes, and skills as they explored the learning environment. Here, the teacher manipulated learning materials related to the topic and asked the students to go through the same thoroughly in their group. In this step, the students got time to think, plan, investigate, and organize the information collected or received by them. The role of the teacher was as a facilitator.

Activity-2

After few minutes, the teacher divided the whole class into some small groups by assigning 5-6 students in each group. During this, the teacher allowed each student of each group to present a solution to the problem. In this stage, each student was encouraged to ask the necessary questions to other students of their groups. So, each student presented solutions to the problem before the group representative and they arrived at the

consensus. After this, the group discussed their procedures to give solutions to the problem, where each member presented his/her procedures before others, and others listened to the presentation, analysed critically, and asked critical questions. At the end of the presentation, the students arrived at the consensus about the procedures of solving the problems. In this stage, the students were encouraged to ask the following questions to themselves individually.

Q1. How did I get my answer?

Q2. What will be other possible solutions to these problems?

Q3. Which strategy is the best to solve this problem?

Q4. How did I arrange the information for solving the problems?

Q5. What kinds of difficulties did you face to solve these problems?

Q6. How did I think about the procedures?

Q7. What are the limitations of this strategy?

During this stage, the students were encouraged to think aloud for finding possible solutions to the problem and work collaboratively. In this stage, the brainstorming method was encouraged.

Explain:

In the third step of teaching, the teacher provided the opportunity to the students for assimilation, where the students tried to connect their previous knowledge with the current learning for the conceptual clarity. Here, more focus was on students' attention on a specific part of engagement and exploration, which helped students to verbalize their conceptual understanding or demonstrating skills.

Activity-3

In this phase, the group representative presented the answers to the given problem before the group and showed a concept map for better visualisation and understanding. The group representatives got equal time to demonstrate their procedure of solving the problem, and the others actively listened to the presenters and posed essential questions to themselves.

Q1. How is this the solution to the problems?

Q2. Are there any other possible solutions?

Q3. Am I able to understand this solution?

Q4. What was running in my mind while listening to the solutions?

Q5. How is my procedure different from others?

During this phase, the teacher also got the opportunity to introduce the definition of the concepts, skills, process, and behaviour. Here, the

teacher encouraged the use of concept mapping strategy among students and assisted them to relate a concept with other sub-concepts in diagrams. The rationale behind the use of concept mapping strategy was to help the students in understanding relationship between concept and sub-concepts relating to the topic. Here the students worked in group to create concept maps related to the topic and showed to each other.

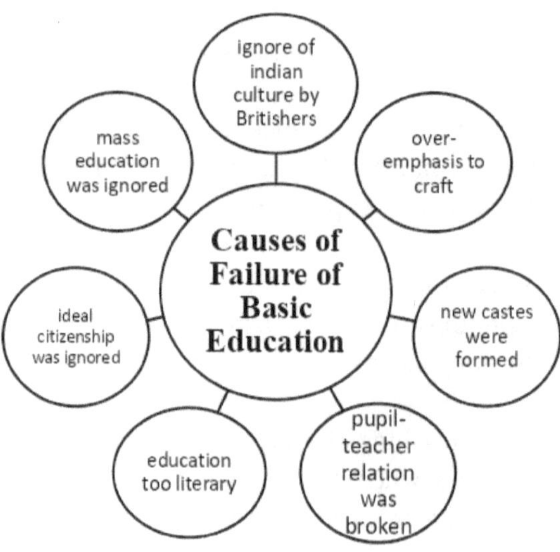

Figure-5: Causes of failure of basic education

The teacher observed the whole process and provided the required assistance wherever required for a better understanding of the students. At the end of this phase, the teacher helped the group to arrive at the consensus of the problem.

Elaborate:

In the fourth step, the focus was given to students' conceptual understanding to allow them for practising different skills and behaviour. Here, the opportunity was provided to the students to apply or extend the previously learned concepts and experiences to the new situations, as a result of which, the students developed better understanding, generated more information, and learned adequate skills. Here, the teacher helped the students to apply their learned knowledge and develop a deeper understanding of the subject matter.

Activity: 4

The teacher gave a question card to the students comprising of analysis-based questions related to the topic and asked them to discuss the possible answers. Here, the teacher brought the attention of the students in front of the class and provided an opportunity to each group representative to present the answers by summarizing the responses of each member of the group. The other students were encouraged to pose essential questions before the group representative. Here, the teacher provided a question card to each group for discussion.

Question Card

Q1. Analyse the status of Basic education in present scenario.

Q2. Is basic education beneficial in present context? Discuss.

Q3. Analyse importance of basic education in rural areas of India and represent your answers in concept maps?

During the whole process, the students were encouraged to think aloud about the questions presented to them and asked them the following questions to themselves.

Q1. How are these questions related to the previous questions?

Q2. How will I use previous information to solve these questions?

Q3. Will I be able to connect my previous knowledge to this problem?

Q4. What kinds of difficulties am I facing to associate previous information?

Q5. What kinds of thoughts are running inside my mind concerned with this problem?

Q6. How can I solve these problems?

The students presented their answers in the group before the group representative, and the representative noted down the responses of each member and summarized the same. Finally, the representative presented the answers before others. The teacher encouraged other students to ask their queries to the representative. In this stage, both thinking-aloud and concept mapping strategies were used.

Evaluate:

In the fifth step i.e., Evaluate, the teacher and students both determined the extent to which the learning and understanding have taken place about the topic, i.e., basic education-II. Here, students were provided an opportunity to review and assess their learning in a summative form. Here, the students were encouraged to assess their understanding, abilities, skills, and behaviour related to the topic. The teacher gave due emphasis on reflection by following both formal and informal assessment procedures rather than traditional quizzes. The teacher gave due importance to self-assessment and writing assignments. The teacher preferred the self-assessment technique in this step, where the students got the opportunity to evaluate their own academic works and learning progress. Through self-assessment, the students got opportunity to identify the gap in their knowledge, track their own progress, set goals, and revise their works.

Activity-5

The teacher favoured some sorts of reflective questions related to the topic before the students and their responses were gathered orally. The reason behind the use of reflective questions was to encourage students for reflecting on their learning skills and generating relevant questions and ideas for propelling future learning experiences. In this stage, the teacher encouraged the students to ask questions about themselves related to their learning activities, processes, and behaviour.

Q1. Did I understand what I need to understand?

Q2. In which condition I learned the most?

Q3. Where did I feel difficulty in understanding the topic?

Q4. How did I learn the subject matter?

Q5. How my learning style is different from others?

Q6. Did I plan properly to adopt procedures for finding the solution to the problems?

Q7. Did I able to learn correctly about basic education-II?

Q8. How did I learn the topic?

Q9. Do I keep in mind the way of my learning? How?

Q10. Am I satisfied with my learning style?

Q11. What is the lacuna in my learning?

Q12. How can I learn better?

The teacher gathered and analysed the responses of the students and measured the learning outcomes of the lesson. The teacher focused on students' abilities to formulate their own meaning and definitions about the topic. Here, the teacher used self-assessment technique.

Homework

At the end of the class, the teachers provided some home works related to the topic discussed before the class. The home works were given based on the students' learning and experience on basic education-II and also, they were instructed to gather information about life philosophy of Gopabandhu Das, which was to be discussed in the next class. So, in this field, the teacher tried to prepare the students independently for the next class considering it as a technique of students' inspiration for further learning activities.

'The core points'- The students developed their deeper understanding regarding the basic education of Gandhiji and constructed new knowledge.

CHAPTER SIX

LIFE PHILOSOPHY OF GOPABANDHU DAS

Lesson Plan-6

School: Higher Secondary School

Class: XII

Subject: Education

Topic: Life Philosophy of Gopabandhu Das

Duration: 1 hour

TLM Required: Education textbook, Laptop to show pictures & Questions

Approach: Constructivist with Metacognitive Interventions

Phases: Engage, Explore, Explain, Elaborate, & Evaluate

Aim and Objective: The objective of this class is to develop understanding among students about life philosophy of Gopabandhu Das.

Learning Outcomes: After the class, the students will be able to

- understand the life philosophy of Gopabandhu
- comprehend implications of life philosophy of Gopabandhu
- demonstrate and evaluate their knowledge in terms of life philosophy of Gopabandhu

Engage:

In the first step of teaching i.e., Engage, the teacher favoured certain activities to capture and stimulate the attention, interest, thinking of the students. Here, the teacher tried to draw the child's curiosity towards learning and keep them mentally engaged in concepts, processes, or skills. So, keeping all these things in mind, the teacher performed the following

activity.

Activity-1

The teacher showed some photographs of famous freedom fighters of Odisha and their activities for the independence of the country, and asked them to share their reflections about the pictures with reference to education. Teacher: *Students, today, we shall make a discussion about* life philosophy of Gopabandhu Das. *What do you know about Gopabandhu Das? What does the life philosophy of Gopabandhu include? What does the life philosophy of Gopabandhu imply?* The teacher allowed each student to answer individually. During this process, the students were instructed to ask the following questions to themselves independently and note down their reflections in their notebook.

Q1. *What do I know about this?*

Q2. *What do I do not know about this?*

Q3. *What kind of question is this?*

Q4. *What do I need to know about these questions?*

Q5. *What should I do to get an idea to answer these questions?*

Q6. *What kind of goal should I set for this?*

Q7. *How can I solve the problem?*

Q8. *Which strategy will help to find a solution to the problem?*

Here, the students were encouraged to think-aloud about the questions asked to them. During the whole process, the thinking-aloud strategy was followed, and the responses of each student were recorded.

Explore:

In the second step of teaching, the teacher provided scope to the students to get involved with the topic and build up their own understanding in groups depending upon the feasibility. In this phase, the students in groups got an opportunity to develop current concepts, processes, and skills as they explored the learning environment. Here, the teacher manipulated learning materials related to the topic and asked the students to go through the same thoroughly in their group. In this step, the students got time to think, plan, investigate, and organize the information collected or received by them. The role of the teacher was as a facilitator.

Activity-2

After few minutes, the teacher divided the whole class into some small groups by assigning 5-6 students in each group. During this, the teacher allowed each student of each group to present a solution to the problem. In this stage, each student was encouraged to ask the necessary questions

to other students of their groups. So, each student presented solutions to the problem before the group representative and they arrived at the consensus. After this, the group discussed their procedures to give solutions to the problem, where each member presented his/her procedures before others, and others listened to the presentation, analysed critically, and asked critical questions. At the end of the presentation, the students arrived at the consensus about the procedures of solving the problems. In this stage, the students were encouraged to ask the following questions to themselves individually.

Q1. How did I get my answer?

Q2. What will be other possible solutions to these problems?

Q3. Which strategy is the best to solve this problem?

Q4. How did I arrange the information for solving the problems?

Q5. What kinds of difficulties did you face to solve these problems?

Q6. How did I think about the procedures?

Q7. What are the limitations of this strategy?

During this stage, the students were encouraged to think aloud for finding possible solutions to the problem and work collaboratively. In this stage, the brainstorming method was encouraged.

Explain:

In the third step of teaching, the teacher provided the opportunity to the students for assimilation, where the students tried to connect their previous knowledge with the current learning for the conceptual clarity. Here, more focus was on students' attention on a specific part of engagement and exploration, which helped students to verbalize their conceptual understanding or demonstrating skills.

Activity-3

In this phase, the teacher encouraged the use of concept mapping. Each group representative discussed with their members of the group and presented the answers to the given problem before the group and showed a concept map for better visualisation and understanding. The group representatives got equal time to demonstrate their procedure of solving the problem, and the others actively listened to the presenters and posed essential questions to themselves.

Q1. How is this the solution to the problems?

Q2. Are there any other possible solutions?

Q3. Am I able to understand this solution?

Q4. What was running in my mind while listening to the solutions?

Q5. How is my procedure different from others?

During this phase, the teacher also got the opportunity to introduce the definition of the concepts, skills, process, and behaviour. Here, the teacher encouraged the use of concept mapping strategy among students and assisted them to relate a concept with other sub-concepts in diagrams. The rationale behind the use of concept mapping strategy was to help the students in understanding relationship between concept and sub-concepts relating to the topic. Here the students worked in group to create concept maps related to the topic and showed to each other.

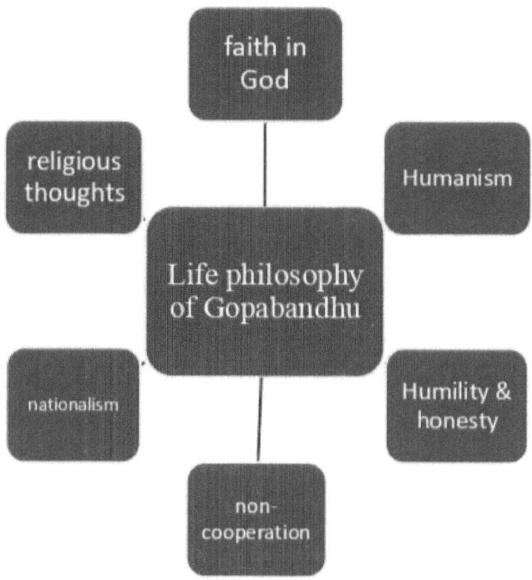

Figure-6: Life philosophy of Gopabandhu

The teacher observed the whole process and provided the required assistance wherever required for a better understanding of the students. At the end of this phase, the teacher helped the group to arrive at the consensus of the problem.

Elaborate:

In the fourth step, the focus was given to students' conceptual understanding to allow them for practising different skills and behaviour. Here, the opportunity was provided to the students to apply or extend the previously learned concepts and experiences to the new situations, as

a result of which, the students developed better understanding, generated more information, and learned adequate skills. Here, the teacher helped the students to apply their learned knowledge and develop a deeper understanding of the subject matter.

Activity: 4

The teacher gave a question card to the students comprising of analysis-based questions related to the topic and asked them to discuss the possible answers. Here, the teacher brought the attention of the students in front of the class and provided an opportunity to each group representative to present the answers by summarizing the responses of each member of the group. The other students were encouraged to pose essential questions before the group representative. Here, the teacher provided a question card to each group for discussion.

Question Card

Q1. Service to humanity is service is God. Elucidate.

Q2. What are the implications of life philosophy of Gopabandhu in 21st century?

Q3. Analyse the key features concerning to life philosophy of Gopabandhu and prepare a concept map.

During the whole process, the students were encouraged to think aloud about the questions presented to them and asked the following questions to themselves.

Q1. How are these questions related to the previous questions?

Q2. How will I use previous information to solve these questions?

Q3. Will I be able to connect my previous knowledge to this problem?

Q4. What kinds of difficulties am I facing to associate previous information?

Q5. What kinds of thoughts are running inside my mind concerned with this problem?

Q6. How can I solve these problems?

The students presented their answers in the group before the group representative, and the representative noted down the responses of each member and summarized the same. Finally, the representative presented the answers before others. The teacher encouraged other students to ask their queries to the representative. In this stage, both thinking-aloud and concept mapping strategies were used.

Evaluate:

In the fifth step i.e., Evaluate, the teacher and students both determined the extent to which the learning and understanding have taken place about

the topic, i.e., Life Philosophy of Gopabandhu. Here, students were provided an opportunity to review and assess their learning in a summative form. Here, the students were encouraged to assess their understanding, abilities, skills, and behaviour related to the topic. The teacher gave due emphasis on reflection by following both formal and informal assessment procedures rather than traditional quizzes. The teacher gave due importance to self-assessment and writing assignments. The teacher preferred the self-assessment technique in this step, where the students got the opportunity to evaluate their own academic works and learning progress. Through self-assessment, the students got opportunity to identify the gap in their knowledge, track their own progress, set goals, and revise their works.

Activity-5

The teacher favoured some sorts of reflective questions related to the topic before the students and their responses were gathered orally. The reason behind the use of reflective questions was to encourage students for reflecting on their learning skills and generating relevant questions and ideas for propelling future learning experiences. In this stage, the teacher encouraged the students to ask questions about themselves related to their learning activities, processes, and behaviour.

Q1. Did I understand what I need to understand?

Q2. In which condition I learned the most?

Q3. Where did I feel difficulty in understanding the topic?

Q4. How did I learn the subject matter?

Q5. How my learning style is different from others?

Q6. Did I plan properly to adopt procedures for finding the solution to the problems?

Q7. Did I able to learn correctly about life philosophy of Gopabandhu?

Q8. How did I learn the topic?

Q9. Do I keep in mind the way of my learning? How?

Q10. Am I satisfied with my learning style?

Q11. What is the lacuna in my learning?

Q12. How can I learn better?

The teacher gathered and analysed the responses of the students and measured the learning outcomes of the lesson. The teacher focused on students' abilities to formulate their own meaning and definitions about the topic. Here, the teacher used self-assessment techniques through this phase.

Homework

At the end of the class, the teachers provided some home works related to the topic discussed before the class. The home works were given based on the students' learning and experience on the life philosophy of Gopabandhu and also, they were instructed to gather information about educational philosophy of Gopabandhu, which was to be discussed in the next class. So, in this field, the teacher tried to prepare the students independently for the next class considering it as a technique of students' inspiration for further learning activities.

'The core points'- The students developed their understanding regarding the life philosophy of Gopabandhu and constructed new knowledge.

CHAPTER SEVEN

EDUCATIONAL PHILOSOPHY OF GOPABANDHU

Lesson Plan-7

School: Higher Secondary School

Class: XII

Subject: Education

Topic: Educational Philosophy of Gopabandhu

Duration: 1 hour

TLM Required: Education textbook, Laptop to show pictures, & Question

Approach: Constructivist with Metacognitive Interventions

Phases: Engage, Explore, Explain, Elaborate, & Evaluate

Aim and Objective: The objective of this class is to develop understanding among students about educational philosophy of Gopabandhu.

Learning Outcomes: After the class, the students will be able to

- understand Gopabandhu's view on concept of education
- comprehend the educational thoughts of Gopabandhu
- demonstrate their knowledge in terms of educational philosophy of Gopabandhu

Engage:

In the first step of teaching i.e., Engage, the teacher favoured certain activities to capture and stimulate the attention, interest, thinking of the

students. Here, the teacher tried to draw the child's curiosity towards learning and keep them mentally engaged in concepts, processes, or skills. So, keeping all these things in mind, the teacher performed the following activity.

Activity-1

The teacher showed some photographs of great Indian and western philosophers like Gandhiji, Tagore, Vivekananda, Gopabandhu, Plato, Pestalozzi, John Dewey, and asked them to share their ideas about their educational contributions. Teacher: *Students, today, we shall make a discussion about educational philosophy of Gopabandhu. What does the educational philosophy of Gopabandhu include? How does Gopabandhu define education and prescribe aims of education?* The teacher allowed each student to answer individually. During this process, the students were instructed to ask the following questions to themselves independently and note down their reflections in their notebook.

Q1. What do I know about this?

Q2. What do I do not know about this?

Q3. What kind of question is this?

Q4. What do I need to know about these questions?

Q5. What should I do to get an idea to answer these questions?

Q6. What kind of goal should I set for this?

Q7. How can I solve the problem?

Q8. Which strategy will help to find a solution to the problem?

Here, the students were encouraged to think-aloud about the questions asked to them. During the whole process, the think-aloud strategy was followed, and the responses of each student were recorded.

Explore:

In the second step of teaching, the teacher provided scope to the students to get involved with the topic and build up their own understanding in groups depending upon the feasibility. In this phase, the students in groups got an opportunity to develop current concepts, processes, and skills as they explored the learning environment. Here, the teacher manipulated learning materials related to the topic and asked the students to go through the same thoroughly in their group. In this step, the students got time to think, plan, investigate, and organize the information collected or received by them. The role of the teacher was as a facilitator.

Activity-2

After few minutes, the teacher divided the whole class into some small groups by assigning 5-6 students in each group. During this, the teacher allowed each student of each group to present a solution to the problem. In this stage, each student was encouraged to ask the necessary questions to other students of their groups. So, each student presented solutions to the problem before the group representative and they arrived at the consensus. After this, the group discussed their procedures to give solutions to the problem, where each member presented his/her procedures before others, and others listened to the presentation, analysed critically, and asked critical questions. At the end of the presentation, the students arrived at the consensus about the procedures of solving the problems. In this stage, the students were encouraged to ask the following questions to themselves individually.

Q1. How did I get my answer?

Q2. What will be other possible solutions to these problems?

Q3. Which strategy is the best to solve this problem?

Q4. How did I arrange the information for solving the problems?

Q5. What kinds of difficulties did you face to solve these problems?

Q6. How did I think about the procedures?

Q7. What are the limitations of this strategy?

During this stage, the students were encouraged to think aloud for finding possible solutions to the problem and work collaboratively. In this stage, the brainstorming method was encouraged.

Explain:

In the third step of teaching, the teacher provided the opportunity to the students for assimilation, where the students tried to connect their previous knowledge with the current learning for the conceptual clarity. Here, more focus was on students' attention on a specific part of engagement and exploration, which helped students to verbalize their conceptual understanding or demonstrating skills.

Activity-3

In this phase, the group representative presented the answers to the given problem before the group and showed a concept map for better visualisation and understanding. The group representatives got equal time to demonstrate their procedure of solving the problem, and the others actively listened to the presenters and posed essential questions to themselves.

Q1. How is this the solution to the problems?

Q2. Are there any other possible solutions?

Q3. Am I able to understand this solution?

Q4. What was running in my mind while listening to the solutions?

Q5. How is my procedure different from others?

During this phase, the teacher also got the opportunity to introduce the definition of the concepts, skills, process, and behaviour. Here, the teacher encouraged the use of concept mapping strategy among students and assisted them to relate a concept with other sub-concepts in diagrams. The rationale behind the use of concept mapping strategy was to help the students in understanding relationship between concept and sub-concepts relating to the topic. Here the students worked in group to create concept maps related to the topic and showed to each other.

Figure-7: Educational thoughts of Gopabandhu

The teacher observed the whole process and provided the required assistance wherever required for a better understanding of the students. At the end of this phase, the teacher helped the group to arrive at the consensus of the problem.

Elaborate:

In the fourth step, the focus was given to students' conceptual understanding to allow them for practising different skills and behaviour.

Here, the opportunity was provided to the students to apply or extend the previously learned concepts and experiences to the new situations, as a result of which, the students developed better understanding, generated more information, and learned adequate skills. Here, the teacher helped the students to apply their learned knowledge and develop a deeper understanding of the subject matter.

Activity: 4

The teacher gave a question card to the students comprising of analysis-based questions related to the topic and asked them to discuss the possible answers. Here, the teacher brought the attention of the students in front of the class and provided an opportunity to each group representative to present the answers by summarizing the responses of each member of the group. The other students were encouraged to pose essential questions before the group representative. Here, the teacher provided a question card to each group for discussion.

Question Card

Q1. Analyse the relevance of educational thoughts of Gopabandhu in present era.

Q2. What is the relevance of open-air schooling prescribed by Gopabandhu?

Q3. Analyse the educational philosophy of Gopabandhu in terms of aims of education and represent in concept maps?

During the whole process, the students were encouraged to think aloud about the questions presented to them and asked them the following questions to themselves.

Q1. How are these questions related to the previous questions?

Q2. How will I use previous information to solve these questions?

Q3. Will I be able to connect my previous knowledge to this problem?

Q4. What kinds of difficulties am I facing to associate previous information?

Q5. What kinds of thoughts are running inside my mind concerned with this problem?

Q6. How can I solve these problems?

The students presented their answers in the group before the group representative, and the representative noted down the responses of each member and summarized the same. Finally, the representative presented the answers before others. The teacher encouraged other students to ask their queries to the representative. In this stage, both thinking-aloud and concept mapping strategies were used.

Evaluate:

In the fifth step i.e., Evaluate, the teacher and students both determined the extent to which the learning and understanding have taken place about the topic, i.e., educational philosophy of Gopabandhu. Here, students were provided an opportunity to review and assess their learning in a summative form. Here, the students were encouraged to assess their understanding, abilities, skills, and behaviour related to the topic. The teacher gave due emphasis on reflection by following both formal and informal assessment procedures rather than traditional quizzes. The teacher gave due importance to self-assessment and writing assignments. The teacher preferred the self-assessment technique in this step, where the students got the opportunity to evaluate their own academic works and learning progress. Through self-assessment, the students got opportunity to identify the gap in their knowledge, track their own progress, set goals, and revise their works.

Activity-5

The teacher favoured some sorts of reflective questions related to the topic before the students and their responses were gathered orally. The reason behind the use of reflective questions was to encourage students for reflecting on their learning skills and generating relevant questions and ideas for propelling future learning experiences. In this stage, the teacher encouraged the students to ask questions about themselves related to their learning activities, processes, and behaviour.

Q1. Did I understand what I need to understand?

Q2. In which condition I learned the most?

Q3. Where did I feel difficulty in understanding the topic?

Q4. How did I learn the subject matter?

Q5. How my learning style is different from others?

Q6. Did I plan properly to adopt procedures for finding the solution to the problems?

Q7. Did I able to learn correctly about educational philosophy of Gopabandhu?

Q8. How did I learn the topic?

Q9. Do I keep in mind the way of my learning? How?

Q10. Am I satisfied with my learning style?

Q11. What is the lacuna in my learning?

Q12. How can I learn better?

The teacher gathered and analysed the responses of the students and measured the learning outcomes of the lesson. The teacher focused on students' abilities to formulate their own meaning and definitions about the topic. Here, the teacher used self-assessment technique.

Homework

At the end of the class, the teachers provided some home works related to the topic discussed before the class. The home works were given based on the students' learning and experience on the educational philosophy of Gopabandhu and also, they were instructed to gather more information about the Satyabadi Banadidyalaya, which was to be discussed in the next class. So, in this field, the teacher tried to prepare the students independently for the next class considering it as a technique of students' inspiration for further learning activities.

'The core points'- The students developed their understanding regarding the educational philosophy of Gopabandhu and constructed new knowledge.

CHAPTER EIGHT

SATYABADI BANAVIDYALAYA-I

Lesson Plan-8

School: Higher Secondary School

Class: XII

Subject: Education

Topic: Satyabadi Banavidyalaya-I

Duration: 1 hour

TLM Required: Education textbook, Laptop to show pictures, & Question

Approach: Constructivist with Metacognitive Interventions

Phases: Engage, Explore, Explain, Elaborate, & Evaluate

Aim and Objective: The objective of this class is to develop understanding among students about Satyabadi Banavidyalaya.

Learning Outcomes: After the class, the students will be able to

- understand the background and feature of Satyabadi Banavidyalaya
- comprehend aims of education and curriculum in Satyabadi Banavidyalaya
- demonstrate their knowledge in terms of Satyabadi Banavidyalaya

Engage:

In the first step of teaching i.e., Engage, the teacher favoured certain activities to capture and stimulate the attention, interest, thinking of the students. Here, the teacher tried to draw the child's curiosity towards learning and keep them mentally engaged in concepts, processes, or skills. So, keeping all these things in mind, the teacher performed the following

activity.

Activity-1

The teacher asked some questions related to the life philosophy of Gopabandhu and asked them to give their view points on educational contributions of Gopabandhu in Indian context. Teacher: *Students, today, we shall make a discussion about Satyabadi Banavidyalaya. What is the background of Satyabadi Banavidyalaya? What are the main features of Satyabadi Banavidyalaya? What were the aims of education and curriculum in Satyabadi System?* The teacher allowed each student to answer individually. During this process, the students were instructed to ask the following questions to themselves independently and note down their reflections in their notebook.

Q1. What do I know about this?

Q2. What do I do not know about this?

Q3. What kind of question is this?

Q4. What do I need to know about these questions?

Q5. What should I do to get an idea to answer these questions?

Q6. What kind of goal should I set for this?

Q7. How can I solve the problem?

Q8. Which strategy will help to find a solution to the problem?

Here, the students were encouraged to think-aloud about the questions asked to them. During the whole process, the thinking-aloud strategy was followed, and the responses of each student were recorded.

Explore:

In the second step of teaching, the teacher provided scope to the students to get involved with the topic and build up their own understanding in groups depending upon the feasibility. In this phase, the students in groups got an opportunity to develop current concepts, processes, and skills as they explored the learning environment. Here, the teacher manipulated learning materials related to the topic and asked the students to go through the same thoroughly in their group. In this step, the students got time to think, plan, investigate, and organize the information collected or received by them. The role of the teacher was as a facilitator.

Activity-2

After few minutes, the teacher divided the whole class into some small groups by assigning 5-6 students in each group. During this, the teacher allowed each student of each group to present a solution to the problem. In this stage, each student was encouraged to ask the necessary questions

to other students of their groups. So, each student presented solutions to the problem before the group representative and they arrived at the consensus. After this, the group discussed their procedures to give solutions to the problem, where each member presented his/her procedures before others, and others listened to the presentation, analysed critically, and asked critical questions. At the end of the presentation, the students arrived at the consensus about the procedures of solving the problems. In this stage, the students were encouraged to ask the following questions to themselves individually.

Q1. How did I get my answer?

Q2. What will be other possible solutions to these problems?

Q3. Which strategy is the best to solve this problem?

Q4. How did I arrange the information for solving the problems?

Q5. What kinds of difficulties did you face to solve these problems?

Q6. How did I think about the procedures?

Q7. What are the limitations of this strategy?

During this stage, the students were encouraged to think aloud for finding possible solutions to the problem and work collaboratively. In this stage, the brainstorming method was encouraged.

Explain:

In the third step of teaching, the teacher provided the opportunity to the students for assimilation, where the students tried to connect their previous knowledge with the current learning for the conceptual clarity. Here, more focus was on students' attention on a specific part of engagement and exploration, which helped students to verbalize their conceptual understanding or demonstrating skills.

Activity-3

In this phase, the group representative presented the answers to the given problem before the group and showed a concept map for better visualisation and understanding. The group representatives got equal time to demonstrate their procedure of solving the problem, and the others actively listened to the presenters and posed essential questions to themselves.

Q1. How is this the solution to the problems?

Q2. Are there any other possible solutions?

Q3. Am I able to understand this solution?

Q4. What was running in my mind while listening to the solutions?

Q5. How is my procedure different from others?

During this phase, the teacher also got the opportunity to introduce the definition of the concepts, skills, process, and behaviour. Here, the teacher encouraged the use of concept mapping strategy among students and assisted them to relate a concept with other sub-concepts in diagrams. The rationale behind the use of concept mapping strategy was to help the students in understanding relationship between concept and sub-concepts relating to the topic. Here the students worked in group to create concept maps related to the topic and showed to each other.

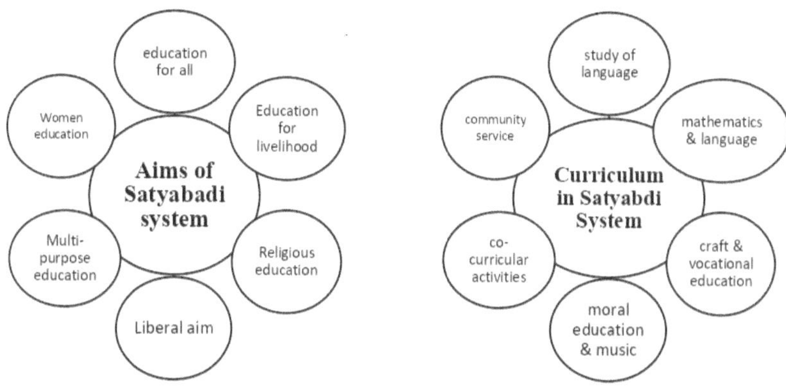

Figure-8: Aims and curriculum of Satyabadi system

The teacher observed the whole process and provided the required assistance wherever required for a better understanding of the students. At the end of this phase, the teacher helped the group to arrive at the consensus of the problem.

Elaborate:

In the fourth step, the focus was given to students' conceptual understanding to allow them for practising different skills and behaviour. Here, the opportunity was provided to the students to apply or extend the previously learned concepts and experiences to the new situations, as a result of which, the students developed better understanding, generated more information, and learned adequate skills. Here, the teacher helped the students to apply their constructed knowledge and develop a deeper understanding of the subject matter.

Activity: 4

The teacher gave a question card to the students comprising of analysis-based questions related to the topic and asked them to discuss the possible answers. Here, the teacher brought the attention of the students in front of the class and provided an opportunity to each group representative to present the answers by summarizing the responses of each member of the group. The other students were encouraged to pose essential questions before the group representative. Here, the teacher provided a question card to each group for discussion.

Question Card

Q1. Analyse the relevance aims of education of Satyabadi Banavidyalaya in present context.

Q2. What is the relevance of curriculum of Satyabadi Banavidyalaya in present context?

Q3. Analyse the main features of basic education in Indian context and represent your answers in concept maps?

During the whole process, the students were encouraged to think aloud about the questions presented to them and asked them the following questions to themselves.

Q1. How are these questions related to the previous questions?

Q2. How will I use previous information to solve these questions?

Q3. Will I be able to connect my previous knowledge to this problem?

Q4. What kinds of difficulties am I facing to associate previous information?

Q5. What kinds of thoughts are running inside my mind concerned with this problem?

Q6. How can I solve these problems?

The students presented their answers in the group before the group representative, and the representative noted down the responses of each member and summarized the same. Finally, the representative presented the answers before others. The teacher encouraged other students to ask their queries to the representative. In this stage, both thinking-aloud and concept mapping strategies were used.

Evaluate:

In the fifth step i.e., Evaluate, the teacher and students both determined the extent to which the learning and understanding have taken place about the topic, i.e., Satyabadi Banavidyalaya-I. Here, students were provided an opportunity to review and assess their learning in a summative form. Here, the students were encouraged to assess their understanding, abilities, skills, and behaviour related to the topic. The teacher gave due emphasis on reflection by following both formal and informal assessment procedures rather than traditional quizzes. The teacher gave due importance to self-assessment and writing assignments. The teacher preferred the self-assessment technique in this step, where the students got the opportunity to evaluate their own academic works and learning progress. Through self-assessment, the students got opportunity to identify the gap in their knowledge, track their own progress, set goals, and revise their works.

Activity-5

The teacher favoured some sorts of reflective questions related to the topic before the students and their responses were gathered orally. The reason behind the use of reflective questions was to encourage students for reflecting on their learning skills and generating relevant questions and ideas for propelling future learning experiences. In this stage, the teacher encouraged the students to ask questions about themselves related to their learning activities, processes, and behaviour.

Q1. Did I understand what I need to understand?

Q2. In which condition I learned the most?

Q3. Where did I feel difficulty in understanding the topic?

Q4. How did I learn the subject matter?

Q5. How my learning style is different from others?

Q6. Did I plan properly to adopt procedures for finding the solution to the problems?

Q7. Did I able to learn correctly about Satyabadi Banavidyalaya-I?

Q8. How did I learn the topic?

Q9. Do I keep in mind the way of my learning? How?

Q10. Am I satisfied with my learning style?

Q11. What is the lacuna in my learning?

Q12. How can I learn better?

The teacher gathered and analysed the responses of the students and measured the learning outcomes of the lesson. The teacher focused on students' abilities to formulate their own meaning and definitions about the topic. Here, the teacher used self-assessment technique.

Homework

At the end of the class, the teachers provided some home works related to the topic discussed before the class. The home works were given based on the students' learning and experience on Satyabadi Banavidyalaya-I and also, they were instructed to gather more information about Satyabadi Banavidyalaya with reference to its methods of teaching, discipline, role of teacher and failure, which was to be discussed in the next class. So, in this field, the teacher tried to prepare the students independently for the next class considering it as a technique of students' inspiration for further learning activities.

'The core points'- The students developed their understanding regarding the educational contribution of Gopabandhu and constructed new knowledge.

CHAPTER NINE

Satyabadi Banavidyalaya-II

Lesson Plan-9

School: Higher Secondary School

Class: XII

Subject: Education

Topic: Satyabadi Banavidyalaya-II

Duration: 1 hour

TLM Required: Education textbook, Laptop to show pictures, & Question

Approach: Constructivist with Metacognitive Interventions

Phases: Engage, Explore, Explain, Elaborate, & Evaluate

Aim and Objective: The objective of this class is to develop deeper understanding among students about Satyabadi Banavidyalaya.

Learning Outcomes: After the class, the students will be able to

- understand the methods of teaching and discipline of Satyabadi Banavidyalaya
- comprehend causes of failure of Satyabadi Banavidyalaya
- demonstrate and evaluate their knowledge in terms of Satyabadi Banavidyalaya

Engage:

In the first step of teaching i.e., Engage, the teacher favoured certain activities to capture and stimulate the attention, interest, thinking of the students. Here, the teacher tried to draw the child's curiosity towards learning and keep them mentally engaged in concepts, processes, or skills.

So, keeping all these things in mind, the teacher performed the following activity.

Activity-1

The teacher asked some questions related to the educational philosophy of Gopabandhu and asked them to give their view points on aims of education and curriculum of Satyabadi Banavidyalaya. Teacher: *Students, today, we shall make a discussion about Satyabadi Banavidyalaya. What were the methods of teaching, discipline, role of teacher in Satyabadi Banavidyalaya? What was the community living in the Satyabadi Banavidyalaya? What were the causes of failure of Satyabadi System?* The teacher allowed each student to answer individually. During this process, the students were instructed to ask the following questions to themselves independently and note down their reflections in their notebook.

Q1. What do I know about this?

Q2. What do I do not know about this?

Q3. What kind of question is this?

Q4. What do I need to know about these questions?

Q5. What should I do to get an idea to answer these questions?

Q6. What kind of goal should I set for this?

Q7. How can I solve the problem?

Q8. Which strategy will help to find a solution to the problem?

Here, the students were encouraged to think-aloud about the questions asked to them. During the whole process, the thinking-aloud strategy was followed, and the responses of each student were recorded.

Explore:

In the second step of teaching, the teacher provided scope to the students to get involved with the topic and build up their own understanding in groups depending upon the feasibility. In this phase, the students in groups got an opportunity to develop current concepts, processes, and skills as they explored the learning environment. Here, the teacher manipulated learning materials related to the topic and asked the students to go through the same thoroughly in their group. In this step, the students got time to think, plan, investigate, and organize the information collected or received by them. The role of the teacher was as a facilitator.

Activity-2

After few minutes, the teacher divided the whole class into some small groups by assigning 5-6 students in each group. During this, the teacher allowed each student of each group to present a solution to the problem.

In this stage, each student was encouraged to ask the necessary questions to other students of their groups. So, each student presented solutions to the problem before the group representative and they arrived at the consensus. After this, the group discussed their procedures to give solutions to the problem, where each member presented his/her procedures before others, and others listened to the presentation, analysed critically, and asked critical questions. At the end of the presentation, the students arrived at the consensus about the procedures of solving the problems. In this stage, the students were encouraged to ask the following questions to themselves individually.

Q1. How did I get my answer?

Q2. What will be other possible solutions to these problems?

Q3. Which strategy is the best to solve this problem?

Q4. How did I arrange the information for solving the problems?

Q5. What kinds of difficulties did you face to solve these problems?

Q6. How did I think about the procedures?

Q7. What are the limitations of this strategy?

During this stage, the students were encouraged to think aloud for finding possible solutions to the problem and work collaboratively. In this stage, the brainstorming method was encouraged.

Explain:

In the third step of teaching, the teacher provided the opportunity to the students for assimilation, where the students tried to connect their previous knowledge with the current learning for the conceptual clarity. Here, more focus was on students' attention on a specific part of engagement and exploration, which helped students to verbalize their conceptual understanding or demonstrating skills.

Activity-3

In this phase, the group representative presented the answers to the given problem before the group and showed a concept map for better visualisation and understanding. The group representatives got equal time to demonstrate their procedure of solving the problem, and the others actively listened to the presenters and posed essential questions to themselves.

Q1. How is this the solution to the problems?

Q2. Are there any other possible solutions?

Q3. Am I able to understand this solution?

Q4. What was running in my mind while listening to the solutions?

Q5. How is my procedure different from others?

During this phase, the teacher also got the opportunity to introduce the definition of the concepts, skills, process, and behaviour. Here, the teacher encouraged the use of concept mapping strategy among students and assisted them to relate a concept with other sub-concepts in diagrams. The rationale behind the use of concept mapping strategy was to help the students in understanding relationship between concept and sub-concepts relating to the topic. Here the students worked in group to create concept maps related to the topic and showed to each other.

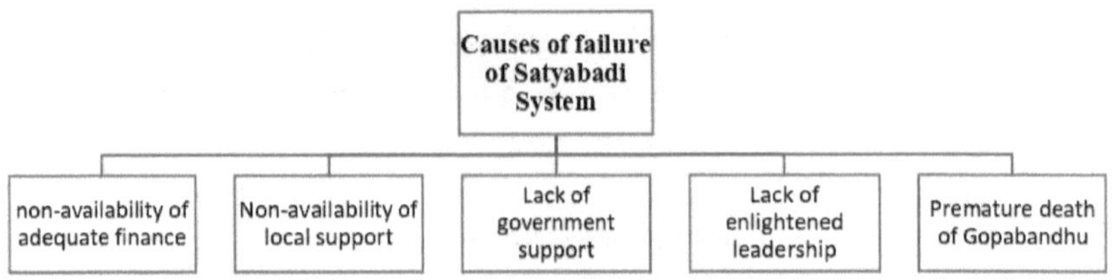

Figure-9: Causes of failure of Satyabadi system

The teacher observed the whole process and provided the required assistance wherever required for a better understanding of the students. At the end of this phase, the teacher helped the group to arrive at the consensus of the problem.

Elaborate:

In the fourth step, the focus was given to students' conceptual understanding to allow them for practising different skills and behaviour. Here, the opportunity was provided to the students to apply or extend the previously learned concepts and experiences to the new situations, as a result of which, the students developed better understanding, generated more information, and learned adequate skills. Here, the teacher helped the students to apply their constructed knowledge and develop a deeper understanding of the subject matter.

Activity: 4

The teacher gave a question card to the students comprising of analysis-based questions related to the topic and asked them to discuss the possible answers. Here, the teacher brought the attention of the students in front of the class and provided an opportunity to each group representative to present the answers by summarizing the responses of each member of the group. The other students were encouraged to pose essential questions before the group representative. Here, the teacher provided a question card to each group for discussion.

Question Card

Q1. Analyse the relevance methods of teaching and discipline of Satyabadi Banavidyalaya in present context.

Q2. What is the relevance of Satyabadi Banavidyalaya in present context?

Q3. Analyse the causes of failure of Satyabadi System and represent your answers in concept maps?

During the whole process, the students were encouraged to think aloud about the questions presented to them and asked them the following questions to themselves.

Q1. How are these questions related to the previous questions?

Q2. How will I use previous information to solve these questions?

Q3. Will I be able to connect my previous knowledge to this problem?

Q4. What kinds of difficulties am I facing to associate previous information?

Q5. What kinds of thoughts are running inside my mind concerned with this problem?

Q6. How can I solve these problems?

The students presented their answers in the group before the group representative, and the representative noted down the responses of each member and summarized the same. Finally, the representative presented the answers before others. The teacher encouraged other students to ask their queries to the representative. In this stage, both thinking-aloud and concept mapping strategies were used.

Evaluate:

In the fifth step i.e., Evaluate, the teacher and students both determined the extent to which the learning and understanding have taken place about the topic, i.e., Satyabadi Banavidyalaya-II. Here, students were provided an opportunity to review and assess their learning in a summative form. Here, the students were encouraged to assess their understanding, abilities, skills, and behaviour related to the topic. The teacher gave due emphasis on reflection by following both formal and informal assessment procedures rather than traditional quizzes. The teacher gave due importance to self-assessment and writing assignments. The teacher preferred the self-assessment technique in this step, where the students got the opportunity to evaluate their own academic works and learning progress. Through self-assessment, the students got opportunity to identify the gap in their knowledge, track their own progress, set goals, and revise their works.

Activity-5

The teacher favoured some sorts of reflective questions related to the topic before the students and their responses were gathered orally. The reason behind the use of reflective questions was to encourage students for reflecting on their learning skills and generating relevant questions and ideas for propelling future learning experiences. In this stage, the teacher encouraged the students to ask questions about themselves related to their learning activities, processes, and behaviour.

Q1. Did I understand what I need to understand?

Q2. In which condition I learned the most?

Q3. Where did I feel difficulty in understanding the topic?

Q4. How did I learn the subject matter?

Q5. How my learning style is different from others?

Q6. Did I plan properly to adopt procedures for finding the solution to the problems?

Q7. Did I able to learn correctly about Satyabadi Banavidyalaya-II?

Q8. How did I learn the topic?

Q9. Do I keep in mind the way of my learning? How?

Q10. Am I satisfied with my learning style?

Q11. What is the lacuna in my learning?

Q12. How can I learn better?

The teacher gathered and analysed the responses of the students and measured the learning outcomes of the lesson. The teacher focused on students' abilities to formulate their own meaning and definitions about the topic. Here, the teacher used self-assessment technique.

Homework

At the end of the class, the teachers provided some home works related to the topic discussed before the class. The home works were given based on the students' learning and experience on Satyabadi Banavidyalaya-I and also, they were instructed to gather information about Rousseau, which was to be discussed in the next class. So, in this field, the teacher tried to prepare the students independently for the next class considering it as a technique of students' inspiration for further learning activities.

'The core points'- The students developed their deeper understanding regarding the educational contribution of Gopabandhu and constructed

new knowledge.

CHAPTER TEN

LIFE PHILOSOPHY OF ROUSSEAU

Lesson Plan-10

School: Higher Secondary School

Class: XII

Subject: Education

Topic: Life Philosophy of Rousseau

Duration: 1 hour

TLM Required: Education textbook, Laptop to show pictures & Questions

Approach: Constructivist with Metacognitive Interventions

Phases: Engage, Explore, Explain, Elaborate, & Evaluate

Aim and Objective: The objective of this class is to develop understanding among students about life philosophy of Rousseau.

Learning Outcomes: After the class, the students will be able to

- understand the life philosophy of Rousseau
- comprehend implications of life philosophy of Rousseau
- demonstrate and evaluate their knowledge in terms of life philosophy of Rousseau

Engage:

In the first step of teaching i.e., Engage, the teacher favoured certain activities to capture and stimulate the attention, interest, thinking of the students. Here, the teacher tried to draw the child's curiosity towards learning and keep them mentally engaged in concepts, processes, or skills. So, keeping all these things in mind, the teacher performed the following

activity.

Activity-1

The teacher showed some photographs of great western philosophers and their educational activities for the dissimilation of knowledge, and asked them to share their reflections about the pictures with reference to educational philosophy. Teacher: *Students, today, we shall make a discussion about* life philosophy of Rousseau. *What do you know about Rousseau? What does the life philosophy of Rousseau include? What does the life philosophy of Rousseau imply?* The teacher allowed each student to answer individually. During this process, the students were instructed to ask the following questions to themselves independently and note down their reflections in their notebook.

Q1. What do I know about this?

Q2. What do I do not know about this?

Q3. What kind of question is this?

Q4. What do I need to know about these questions?

Q5. What should I do to get an idea to answer these questions?

Q6. What kind of goal should I set for this?

Q7. How can I solve the problem?

Q8. Which strategy will help to find a solution to the problem?

Here, the students were encouraged to think-aloud about the questions asked to them. During the whole process, the think-aloud strategy was followed, and the responses of each student were recorded.

Explore:

In the second step of teaching, the teacher provided scope to the students to get involved with the topic and build up their own understanding in groups depending upon the feasibility. In this phase, the students in groups got an opportunity to develop current concepts, processes, and skills as they explored the learning environment. Here, the teacher manipulated learning materials related to the topic and asked the students to go through the same thoroughly in their group. In this step, the students got time to think, plan, investigate, and organize the information collected or received by them. The role of the teacher was as a facilitator.

Activity-2

After few minutes, the teacher divided the whole class into some small groups by assigning 5-6 students in each group. During this, the teacher allowed each student of each group to present a solution to the problem. In this stage, each student was encouraged to ask the necessary questions

to other students of their groups. So, each student presented solutions to the problem before the group representative and they arrived at the consensus. After this, the group discussed their procedures to give solutions to the problem, where each member presented his/her procedures before others, and others listened to the presentation, analysed critically, and asked critical questions. At the end of the presentation, the students arrived at the consensus about the procedures of solving the problems. In this stage, the students were encouraged to ask the following questions to themselves individually.

Q1. How did I get my answer?

Q2. What will be other possible solutions to these problems?

Q3. Which strategy is the best to solve this problem?

Q4. How did I arrange the information for solving the problems?

Q5. What kinds of difficulties did you face to solve these problems?

Q6. How did I think about the procedures?

Q7. What are the limitations of this strategy?

During this stage, the students were encouraged to think aloud for finding possible solutions to the problem and work collaboratively. In this stage, the brainstorming method was encouraged.

Explain:

In the third step of teaching, the teacher provided the opportunity to the students for assimilation, where the students tried to connect their previous knowledge with the current learning for the conceptual clarity. Here, more focus was on students' attention on a specific part of engagement and exploration, which helped students to verbalize their conceptual understanding or demonstrating skills.

Activity-3

In this phase, the teacher encouraged the use of concept mapping. Each group representative discussed with their members of the group and presented the answers to the given problem before the group and showed a concept map for better visualisation and understanding. The group representatives got equal time to demonstrate their procedure of solving the problem, and the others actively listened to the presenters and posed essential questions to themselves.

Q1. How is this the solution to the problems?

Q2. Are there any other possible solutions?

Q3. Am I able to understand this solution?

Q4. What was running in my mind while listening to the solutions?

Q5. How is my procedure different from others?

During this phase, the teacher also got the opportunity to introduce the definition of the concepts, skills, process, and behaviour. Here, the teacher encouraged the use of concept mapping strategy among students and assisted them to relate a concept with other sub-concepts in diagrams. The rationale behind the use of concept mapping strategy was to help the students in understanding relationship between concept and sub-concepts relating to the topic. Here the students worked in group to create concept maps related to the topic and showed to each other.

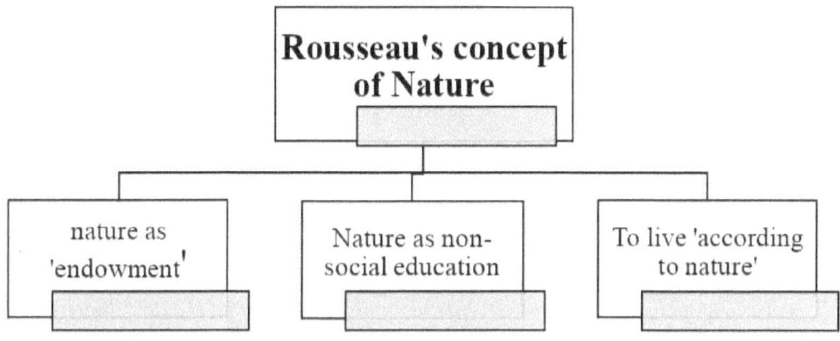

Figure-10: Rousseau's concept of nature

The teacher observed the whole process and provided the required assistance wherever required for a better understanding of the students. At the end of this phase, the teacher helped the group to arrive at the consensus of the problem.

Elaborate:

In the fourth step, the focus was given to students' conceptual understanding to allow them for practising different skills and behaviour. Here, the opportunity was provided to the students to apply or extend the previously learned concepts and experiences to the new situations, as a result of which, the students developed better understanding, generated more information, and learned adequate skills. Here, the teacher helped the students to apply their learned knowledge and develop a deeper understanding of the subject matter.

Activity: 4

The teacher gave a question card to the students comprising of analysis-based questions related to the topic and asked them to discuss the possible answers. Here, the teacher brought the attention of the students in front of the class and provided an opportunity to each group representative to present the answers by summarizing the responses of each member of the group. The other students were encouraged to pose essential questions before the group representative. Here, the teacher provided a question card to each group for discussion.

Question Card

Q1. Return to nature. Elucidate.

Q2. What are the implications of life philosophy of Rousseau in 21st century?

Q3. Analyse the concept of nature described by Rousseau and prepare a concept map.

During the whole process, the students were encouraged to think aloud about the questions presented to them and asked them the following questions to themselves.

Q1. How are these questions related to the previous questions?

Q2. How will I use previous information to solve these questions?

Q3. Will I be able to connect my previous knowledge to this problem?

Q4. What kinds of difficulties am I facing to associate previous information?

Q5. What kinds of thoughts are running inside my mind concerned with this problem?

Q6. How can I solve these problems?

The students presented their answers in the group before the group representative, and the representative noted down the responses of each member and summarized the same. Finally, the representative presented the answers before others. The teacher encouraged other students to ask their queries to the representative. In this stage, both thinking-aloud and concept mapping strategies were used.

Evaluate:

In the fifth step i.e., Evaluate, the teacher and students both determined the extent to which the learning and understanding have taken place about the topic, i.e., Life Philosophy of Rosseau. Here, students were provided an opportunity to review and assess their learning in a summative form. Here, the students were encouraged to assess their understanding, abilities, skills, and behaviour related to the topic. The teacher gave due emphasis on reflection by following both formal and informal assessment procedures rather than traditional quizzes. The teacher gave due importance to self-assessment and writing assignments. The teacher preferred the self-assessment technique in this step, where the students got the opportunity to evaluate their own academic works and learning progress. Through self-assessment, the students got opportunity to identify the gap in their knowledge, track their own progress, set goals, and revise their works.

Activity-5

The teacher favoured some sorts of reflective questions related to the topic before the students and their responses were gathered orally. The reason behind the use of reflective questions was to encourage students for reflecting on their learning skills and generating relevant questions and ideas for propelling future learning experiences. In this stage, the teacher encouraged the students to ask questions about themselves related to their learning activities, processes, and behaviour.

Q1. Did I understand what I need to understand?

Q2. In which condition I learned the most?

Q3. Where did I feel difficulty in understanding the topic?

Q4. How did I learn the subject matter?

Q5. How my learning style is different from others?

Q6. Did I plan properly to adopt procedures for finding the solution to the problems?

Q7. Did I able to learn correctly about life philosophy of Rosseau?

Q8. How did I learn the topic?

Q9. Do I keep in mind the way of my learning? How?

Q10. Am I satisfied with my learning style?

Q11. What is the lacuna in my learning?

Q12. How can I learn better?

The teacher gathered and analysed the responses of the students and measured the learning outcomes of the lesson. The teacher focused on students' abilities to formulate their own meaning and definitions about the topic. Here, the teacher used self-assessment techniques through this phase.

Homework

At the end of the class, the teachers provided some home works related to the topic discussed before the class. The home works were given based on the students' learning and experience on the life philosophy of Rousseau and also, they were instructed to gather information about educational philosophy of Rousseau, which was to be discussed in the next class. So, in this field, the teacher tried to prepare the students independently for the next class considering it as a technique of students' inspiration for further learning activities.

'The core points'- The students developed their understanding regarding the life philosophy of Rousseau and constructed new knowledge.

CHAPTER ELEVEN

EDUCATIONAL PHILOSOPHY OF ROUSSEAU-I

Lesson Plan-11

School: Higher Secondary School

Class: XII

Subject: Education

Topic: Educational Philosophy of Rousseau-I

Duration: 1 hour

TLM Required: Education textbook, Laptop to show pictures, & Question

Approach: Constructivist with Metacognitive Interventions

Phases: Engage, Explore, Explain, Elaborate, & Evaluate

Aim and Objective: The objective of this class is to develop understanding among students about educational philosophy of Rousseau.

Learning Outcomes: After the class, the students will be able to

- understand Rousseau's view on concept of education
- comprehend aims of education and negative education as prescribed by Rousseau
- demonstrate and evaluate their knowledge in terms of educational philosophy of Rousseau

Engage:

In the first step of teaching i.e., Engage, the teacher favoured certain activities to capture and stimulate the attention, interest, thinking of the

students. Here, the teacher tried to draw the child's curiosity towards learning and keep them mentally engaged in concepts, processes, or skills. So, keeping all these things in mind, the teacher performed the following activity.

Activity-1

The teacher showed some photographs of great Indian and western philosophers like Gandhiji, Tagore, Vivekananda, Plato, Pestalozzi, Rousseau, John Dewey, and asked them to share their ideas about the educational contributions of the philosophers. Teacher: *Students, today, we shall make a discussion about educational philosophy of Rousseau with reference to concept of education, aims of education and negative education. What does the educational philosophy of Rousseau include? How does Rousseau define education and prescribe aims of education? What is negative education according to Rousseau?* The teacher allowed each student to answer individually. During this process, the students were instructed to ask the following questions to themselves independently and note down their reflections in their notebook.

Q1. What do I know about this?

Q2. What do I do not know about this?

Q3. What kind of question is this?

Q4. What do I need to know about these questions?

Q5. What should I do to get an idea to answer these questions?

Q6. What kind of goal should I set for this?

Q7. How can I solve the problem?

Q8. Which strategy will help to find a solution to the problem?

Here, the students were encouraged to think-aloud about the questions asked to them. During the whole process, the think-aloud strategy was followed, and the responses of each student were recorded.

Explore:

In the second step of teaching, the teacher provided scope to the students to get involved with the topic and build up their own understanding in groups depending upon the feasibility. In this phase, the students in groups got an opportunity to develop current concepts, processes, and skills as they explored the learning environment. Here, the teacher manipulated learning materials related to the topic and asked the students to go through the same thoroughly in their group. In this step, the students got time to think, plan, investigate, and organize the information collected or received by them. The role of the teacher was as a facilitator.

Activity-2

After few minutes, the teacher divided the whole class into some small groups by assigning 5-6 students in each group. During this, the teacher allowed each student of each group to present a solution to the problem. In this stage, each student was encouraged to ask the necessary questions to other students of their groups. So, each student presented solutions to the problem before the group representative and they arrived at the consensus. After this, the group discussed their procedures to give solutions to the problem, where each member presented his/her procedures before others, and others listened to the presentation, analysed critically, and asked critical questions. At the end of the presentation, the students arrived at the consensus about the procedures of solving the problems. In this stage, the students were encouraged to ask the following questions to themselves individually.

Q1. How did I get my answer?

Q2. What will be other possible solutions to these problems?

Q3. Which strategy is the best to solve this problem?

Q4. How did I arrange the information for solving the problems?

Q5. What kinds of difficulties did you face to solve these problems?

Q6. How did I think about the procedures?

Q7. What are the limitations of this strategy?

During this stage, the students were encouraged to think aloud for finding possible solutions to the problem and work collaboratively. In this stage, the brainstorming method was encouraged.

Explain:

In the third step of teaching, the teacher provided the opportunity to the students for assimilation, where the students tried to connect their previous knowledge with the current learning for the conceptual clarity. Here, more focus was on students' attention on a specific part of engagement and exploration, which helped students to verbalize their conceptual understanding or demonstrating skills.

Activity-3

In this phase, the group representative presented the answers to the given problem before the group and showed a concept map for better visualisation and understanding. The group representatives got equal time to demonstrate their procedure of solving the problem, and the others actively listened to the presenters and posed essential questions to themselves.

Q1. How is this the solution to the problems?

Q2. Are there any other possible solutions?

Q3. Am I able to understand this solution?

Q4. What was running in my mind while listening to the solutions?

Q5. How is my procedure different from others?

During this phase, the teacher also got the opportunity to introduce the definition of the concepts, skills, process, and behaviour. Here, the teacher encouraged the use of concept mapping strategy among students and assisted them to relate a concept with other sub-concepts in diagrams. The rationale behind the use of concept mapping strategy was to help the students in understanding relationship between concept and sub-concepts relating to the topic. Here the students worked in group to create concept maps related to the topic and showed to each other.

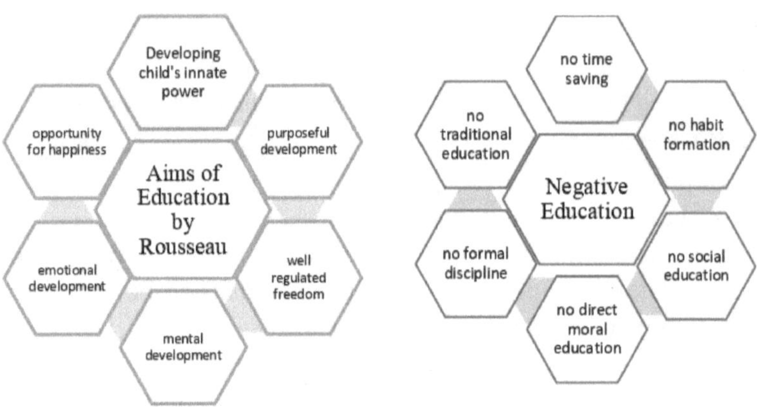

Figure-11: Aims of education and negative education by Rousseau

The teacher observed the whole process and provided the required assistance wherever required for a better understanding of the students. At the end of this phase, the teacher helped the group to arrive at the consensus of the problem.

Elaborate:

In the fourth step, the focus was given to students' conceptual understanding to allow them for practising different skills and behaviour. Here, the opportunity was provided to the students to apply or extend the previously learned concepts and experiences to the new situations, as

a result of which, the students developed better understanding, generated more information, and learned adequate skills. Here, the teacher helped the students to apply their learned knowledge and develop a deeper understanding of the subject matter.

Activity: 4

The teacher gave a question card to the students comprising of analysis-based questions related to the topic and asked them to discuss the possible answers. Here, the teacher brought the attention of the students in front of the class and provided an opportunity to each group representative to present the answers by summarizing the responses of each member of the group. The other students were encouraged to pose essential questions before the group representative. Here, the teacher provided a question card to each group for discussion.

Question Card

Q1. Analyse the relevance of aims of education prescribed by Rousseau in present era.

Q2. Analyse the concept of education given by Rousseau and find key points?

Q3. Analyse the concept of negative education and its implications for present context and represent in concept maps?

During the whole process, the students were encouraged to think aloud about the questions presented to them and asked them the following questions to themselves.

Q1. How are these questions related to the previous questions?

Q2. How will I use previous information to solve these questions?

Q3. Will I be able to connect my previous knowledge to this problem?

Q4. What kinds of difficulties am I facing to associate previous information?

Q5. What kinds of thoughts are running inside my mind concerned with this problem?

Q6. How can I solve these problems?

The students presented their answers in the group before the group representative, and the representative noted down the responses of each member and summarized the same. Finally, the representative presented the answers before others. The teacher encouraged other students to ask their queries to the representative. In this stage, both thinking-aloud and concept mapping strategies were used.

Evaluate:

In the fifth step i.e., Evaluate, the teacher and students both determined the extent to which the learning and understanding have taken place about

the topic, i.e., educational philosophy of Rousseau-I. Here, students were provided an opportunity to review and assess their learning in a summative form. Here, the students were encouraged to assess their understanding, abilities, skills, and behaviour related to the topic. The teacher gave due emphasis on reflection by following both formal and informal assessment procedures rather than traditional quizzes. The teacher gave due importance to self-assessment and writing assignments. The teacher preferred the self-assessment technique in this step, where the students got the opportunity to evaluate their own academic works and learning progress. Through self-assessment, the students got opportunity to identify the gap in their knowledge, track their own progress, set goals, and revise their works.

Activity-5

The teacher favoured some sorts of reflective questions related to the topic before the students and their responses were gathered orally. The reason behind the use of reflective questions was to encourage students for reflecting on their learning skills and generating relevant questions and ideas for propelling future learning experiences. In this stage, the teacher encouraged the students to ask questions about themselves related to their learning activities, processes, and behaviour.

Q1. Did I understand what I need to understand?

Q2. In which condition I learned the most?

Q3. Where did I feel difficulty in understanding the topic?

Q4. How did I learn the subject matter?

Q5. How my learning style is different from others?

Q6. Did I plan properly to adopt procedures for finding the solution to the problems?

Q7. Did I able to learn correctly about educational philosophy of Rousseau-I?

Q8. How did I learn the topic?

Q9. Do I keep in mind the way of my learning? How?

Q10. Am I satisfied with my learning style?

Q11. What is the lacuna in my learning?

Q12. How can I learn better?

The teacher gathered and analysed the responses of the students and measured the learning outcomes of the lesson. The teacher focused on students' abilities to formulate their own meaning and definitions about the topic. Here, the teacher used self-assessment technique.

Homework

At the end of the class, the teachers provided some home works related to the topic discussed before the class. The home works were given based on the students' learning and experience on the educational philosophy of Rousseau-I and also, they were instructed to gather more information about the educational philosophy of Rousseau with reference to curriculum and methods of teaching, which was to be discussed in the next class. So, in this field, the teacher tried to prepare the students independently for the next class considering it as a technique of students' inspiration for further learning activities.

'The core points'- The students developed their understanding regarding the life philosophy of Rousseau and constructed new knowledge.

CHAPTER TWELVE

EDUCATIONAL PHILOSOPHY OF ROUSSEAU-II

Lesson Plan-12

School: Higher Secondary School

Class: XII

Subject: Education

Topic: Educational Philosophy of Rousseau-II

Duration: 1 hour

TLM Required: Education textbook, Laptop to show pictures, & Question

Approach: Constructivist with Metacognitive Interventions

Phases: Engage, Explore, Explain, Elaborate, & Evaluate

Aim and Objective: The objective of this class is to develop deeper understanding among students about educational philosophy of Rousseau.

Learning Outcomes: After the class, the students will be able to

- understand Rousseau's view on curriculum
- comprehend methods of teaching as prescribed by Rousseau
- demonstrate and evaluate their knowledge in terms of educational philosophy of Rousseau

Engage:

In the first step of teaching i.e., Engage, the teacher favoured certain activities to capture and stimulate the attention, interest, thinking of the students. Here, the teacher tried to draw the child's curiosity towards learning and keep them mentally engaged in concepts, processes, or skills. So, keeping all these things in mind, the teacher performed the following activity.

Activity-1

The teacher showed some photographs of Rousseau, and asked them to share their ideas about their educational philosophy of Rousseau with reference to concept of education, aims of education and negative education with examples. Teacher: *Students, today, we shall make a discussion about educational philosophy of Rousseau with reference to curriculum and methods of teaching. What kind curriculum Rousseau has prescribed? What are the methods of teaching prescribed by Rousseau?* The teacher allowed each student to answer individually. During this process, the students were instructed to ask the following questions to themselves independently and note down their reflections in their notebook.

Q1. What do I know about this?

Q2. What do I do not know about this?

Q3. What kind of question is this?

Q4. What do I need to know about these questions?

Q5. What should I do to get an idea to answer these questions?

Q6. What kind of goal should I set for this?

Q7. How can I solve the problem?

Q8. Which strategy will help to find a solution to the problem?

Here, the students were encouraged to think-aloud about the questions asked to them. During the whole process, the think-aloud strategy was followed, and the responses of each student were recorded.

Explore:

In the second step of teaching, the teacher provided scope to the students to get involved with the topic and build up their own understanding in groups depending upon the feasibility. In this phase, the students in groups got an opportunity to develop current concepts, processes, and skills as they explored the learning environment. Here, the teacher manipulated learning materials related to the topic and asked the students to go through the same thoroughly in their group. In this step, the students got time to think, plan, investigate, and organize the information collected or received by them. The role of the teacher was as a facilitator.

Activity-2

After few minutes, the teacher divided the whole class into some small groups by assigning 5-6 students in each group. During this, the teacher allowed each student of each group to present a solution to the problem. In this stage, each student was encouraged to ask the necessary questions to other students of their groups. So, each student presented solutions to the problem before the group representative and they arrived at the consensus. After this, the group discussed their procedures to give solutions to the problem, where each member presented his/her procedures before others, and others listened to the presentation, analysed critically, and asked critical questions. At the end of the presentation, the students arrived at the consensus about the procedures of solving the problems. In this stage, the students were encouraged to ask the following questions to themselves individually.

Q1. How did I get my answer?

Q2. What will be other possible solutions to these problems?

Q3. Which strategy is the best to solve this problem?

Q4. How did I arrange the information for solving the problems?

Q5. What kinds of difficulties did you face to solve these problems?

Q6. How did I think about the procedures?

Q7. What are the limitations of this strategy?

During this stage, the students were encouraged to think aloud for finding possible solutions to the problem and work collaboratively. In this stage, the brainstorming method was encouraged.

Explain:

In the third step of teaching, the teacher provided the opportunity to the students for assimilation, where the students tried to connect their previous knowledge with the current learning for the conceptual clarity. Here, more focus was on students' attention on a specific part of engagement and exploration, which helped students to verbalize their conceptual understanding or demonstrating skills.

Activity-3

In this phase, the group representative presented the answers to the given problem before the group and showed a concept map for better visualisation and understanding. The group representatives got equal time to demonstrate their procedure of solving the problem, and the others actively listened to the presenters and posed essential questions to themselves.

Q1. How is this the solution to the problems?

Q2. Are there any other possible solutions?

Q3. Am I able to understand this solution?

Q4. What was running in my mind while listening to the solutions?

Q5. How is my procedure different from others?

During this phase, the teacher also got the opportunity to introduce the definition of the concepts, skills, process, and behaviour. Here, the teacher encouraged the use of concept mapping strategy among students and assisted them to relate a concept with other sub-concepts in diagrams. The rationale behind the use of concept mapping strategy was to help the students in understanding relationship between concept and sub-concepts relating to the topic. Here the students worked in group to create concept maps related to the topic and showed to each other.

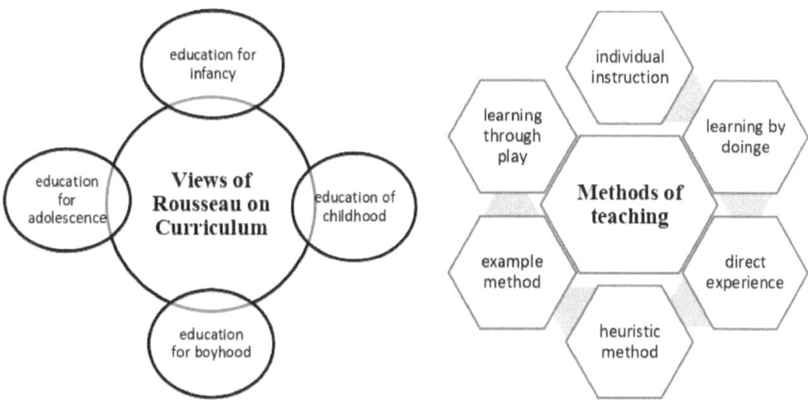

Figure-12: Views of Rousseau on curriculum and methods of teaching

The teacher observed the whole process and provided the required assistance wherever required for a better understanding of the students. At the end of this phase, the teacher helped the group to arrive at the consensus of the problem.

Elaborate:

In the fourth step, the focus was given to students' conceptual understanding to allow them for practising different skills and behaviour. Here, the opportunity was provided to the students to apply or extend the previously learned concepts and experiences to the new situations, as a result of which, the students developed better understanding, generated more information, and learned adequate skills. Here, the teacher helped the students to apply their learned knowledge and develop a deeper understanding of the subject matter.

Activity: 4

The teacher gave a question card to the students comprising of analysis-based questions related to the topic and asked them to discuss the possible answers. Here, the teacher brought the attention of the students in front of the class and provided an opportunity to each group representative to present the answers by summarizing the responses of each member of the group. The other students were encouraged to pose essential questions before the group representative. Here, the teacher provided a question card to each group for discussion.

Question Card

Q1. What is the relevance of curriculum prescribed by Rousseau in present era?

Q2. Analyse the methods of teaching prescribed by Rousseau and their implications for the present scenario.

Q3. Analyse the educational philosophy of Rousseau in terms of curriculum and methods of teaching and represent in concept maps.

During the whole process, the students were encouraged to think aloud about the questions presented to them and asked them the following questions to themselves.

Q1. How are these questions related to the previous questions?

Q2. How will I use previous information to solve these questions?

Q3. Will I be able to connect my previous knowledge to this problem?

Q4. What kinds of difficulties am I facing to associate previous information?

Q5. What kinds of thoughts are running inside my mind concerned with this problem?

Q6. How can I solve these problems?

The students presented their answers in the group before the group representative, and the representative noted down the responses of each member and summarized the same. Finally, the representative presented the answers before others. The teacher encouraged other students to ask their queries to the representative. In this stage, both thinking-aloud and concept mapping strategies were used.

Evaluate:

In the fifth step i.e., Evaluate, the teacher and students both determined the extent to which the learning and understanding have taken place about the topic, i.e., educational philosophy of Rousseau-II. Here, students were provided an opportunity to review and assess their learning in a summative form. Here, the students were encouraged to assess their understanding, abilities, skills, and behaviour related to the topic. The teacher gave due emphasis on reflection by following both formal and informal assessment procedures rather than traditional quizzes. The teacher gave due importance to self-assessment and writing assignments. The teacher preferred the self-assessment technique in this step, where the students got the opportunity to evaluate their own academic works and learning progress. Through self-assessment, the students got opportunity to identify the gap in their knowledge, track their own progress, set goals, and revise their works.

Activity-5

The teacher favoured some sorts of reflective questions related to the topic before the students and their responses were gathered orally. The reason behind the use of reflective questions was to encourage students for reflecting on their learning skills and generating relevant questions and ideas for propelling future learning experiences. In this stage, the teacher encouraged the students to ask questions about themselves related to their learning activities, processes, and behaviour.

Q1. Did I understand what I need to understand?

Q2. In which condition I learned the most?

Q3. Where did I feel difficulty in understanding the topic?

Q4. How did I learn the subject matter?

Q5. How my learning style is different from others?

Q6. Did I plan properly to adopt procedures for finding the solution to the problems?

Q7. Did I able to learn correctly about educational philosophy of Rousseau-II?

Q8. How did I learn the topic?

Q9. Do I keep in mind the way of my learning? How?

Q10. Am I satisfied with my learning style?

Q11. What is the lacuna in my learning?

Q12. How can I learn better?

The teacher gathered and analysed the responses of the students and measured the learning outcomes of the lesson. The teacher focused on students' abilities to formulate their own meaning and definitions about the topic. Here, the teacher used self-assessment technique.

Homework

At the end of the class, the teachers provided some home works related to the topic discussed before the class. The home works were given based on the students' learning and experience on the educational philosophy of Rousseau-II and also, they were instructed to gather more information about the educational philosophy of Rousseau with reference to role of teacher, discipline and contribution of Rousseau, which was to be discussed in the next class. So, in this field, the teacher tried to prepare the students independently for the next class considering it as a technique of students' inspiration for further learning activities.

'The core points'- The students developed their understanding regarding the educational philosophy of Rousseau and constructed new knowledge.

CHAPTER THIRTEEN

EDUCATIONAL PHILOSOPHY OF ROUSSEAU-III

Lesson Plan-13

School: Higher Secondary School

Class: XII

Subject: Education

Topic: Educational Philosophy of Rousseau-III

Duration: 1 hour

TLM Required: Education textbook, Laptop to show pictures, & Question

Approach: Constructivist with Metacognitive Interventions

Phases: Engage, Explore, Explain, Elaborate, & Evaluate

Aim and Objective: The objective of this class is to develop deeper understanding among students about educational philosophy of Rousseau.

Learning Outcomes: After the class, the students will be able to

- understand Rousseau's view on role of teacher and discipline
- comprehend the contributions of Rousseau to education
- demonstrate and evaluate their knowledge in terms of educational philosophy of Rousseau

Engage:

In the first step of teaching i.e., Engage, the teacher favoured certain activities to capture and stimulate the attention, interest, thinking of the students. Here, the teacher tried to draw the child's curiosity towards learning and keep them mentally engaged in concepts, processes, or skills. So, keeping all these things in mind, the teacher performed the following activity.

Activity-1

The teacher showed some photographs of Rousseau, and asked them to share their ideas about their educational philosophy of Rousseau with reference to curriculum and methods of teaching with suitable examples. Teacher: *Students, today, we shall make a discussion about educational philosophy of Rousseau with reference to role of teacher, discipline and educational contributions. What was the views of Rousseau on the role of teacher? What is the view of Rousseau on discipline in education? What are the major educational contributions of Rousseau?* The teacher allowed each student to answer individually. During this process, the students were instructed to ask the following questions to themselves independently and note down their reflections in their notebook.

Q1. What do I know about this?

Q2. What do I do not know about this?

Q3. What kind of question is this?

Q4. What do I need to know about these questions?

Q5. What should I do to get an idea to answer these questions?

Q6. What kind of goal should I set for this?

Q7. How can I solve the problem?

Q8. Which strategy will help to find a solution to the problem?

Here, the students were encouraged to think-aloud about the questions asked to them. During the whole process, the think-aloud strategy was followed, and the responses of each student were recorded.

Explore:

In the second step of teaching, the teacher provided scope to the students to get involved with the topic and build up their own understanding in groups depending upon the feasibility. In this phase, the students in groups got an opportunity to develop current concepts, processes, and skills as they explored the learning environment. Here, the teacher manipulated learning materials related to the topic and asked the students to go through the same thoroughly in their group. In this step, the students got time to think, plan, investigate, and organize the information collected or received by them. The role of the teacher was as a facilitator.

Activity-2

After few minutes, the teacher divided the whole class into some small groups by assigning 5-6 students in each group. During this, the teacher allowed each student of each group to present a solution to the problem. In this stage, each student was encouraged to ask the necessary questions to other students of their groups. So, each student presented solutions to the problem before the group representative and they arrived at the consensus. After this, the group discussed their procedures to give solutions to the problem, where each member presented his/her procedures before others, and others listened to the presentation, analysed critically, and asked critical questions. At the end of the presentation, the students arrived at the consensus about the procedures of solving the problems. In this stage, the students were encouraged to ask the following questions to themselves individually.

Q1. How did I get my answer?

Q2. What will be other possible solutions to these problems?

Q3. Which strategy is the best to solve this problem?

Q4. How did I arrange the information for solving the problems?

Q5. What kinds of difficulties did you face to solve these problems?

Q6. How did I think about the procedures?

Q7. What are the limitations of this strategy?

During this stage, the students were encouraged to think aloud for finding possible solutions to the problem and work collaboratively. In this stage, the brainstorming method was encouraged.

Explain:

In the third step of teaching, the teacher provided the opportunity to the students for assimilation, where the students tried to connect their previous knowledge with the current learning for the conceptual clarity. Here, more focus was on students' attention on a specific part of engagement and exploration, which helped students to verbalize their conceptual understanding or demonstrating skills.

Activity-3

In this phase, the group representative presented the answers to the given problem before the group and showed a concept map for better visualisation and understanding. The group representatives got equal time to demonstrate their procedure of solving the problem, and the others actively listened to the presenters and posed essential questions to themselves.

Q1. How is this the solution to the problems?

Q2. Are there any other possible solutions?

Q3. Am I able to understand this solution?

Q4. What was running in my mind while listening to the solutions?

Q5. How is my procedure different from others?

During this phase, the teacher also got the opportunity to introduce the definition of the concepts, skills, process, and behaviour. Here, the teacher encouraged the use of concept mapping strategy among students and assisted them to relate a concept with other sub-concepts in diagrams. The rationale behind the use of concept mapping strategy was to help the students in understanding relationship between concept and sub-concepts relating to the topic. Here the students worked in group to create concept maps related to the topic and showed to each other.

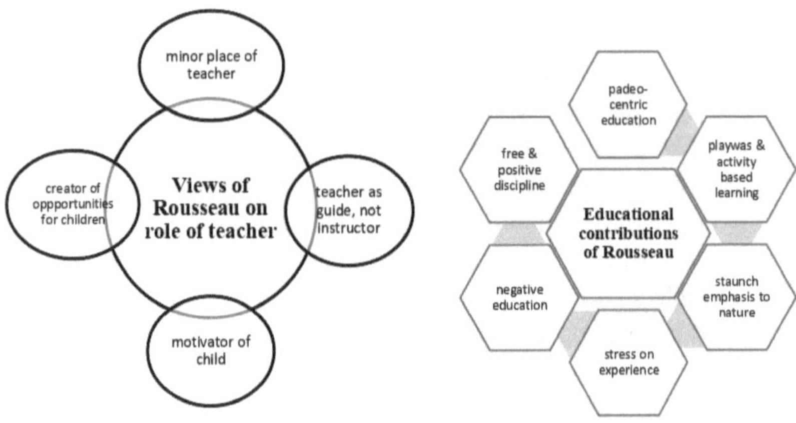

Figure-13: Educational philosophy and views of Rousseau on role of teacher

The teacher observed the whole process and provided the required assistance wherever required for a better understanding of the students. At the end of this phase, the teacher helped the group to arrive at the consensus of the problem.

Elaborate:

In the fourth step, the focus was given to students' conceptual understanding to allow them for practising different skills and behaviour. Here, the opportunity was provided to the students to apply or extend the previously learned concepts and experiences to the new situations, as

a result of which, the students developed better understanding, generated more information, and learned adequate skills. Here, the teacher helped the students to apply their learned knowledge and develop a deeper understanding of the subject matter.

Activity: 4

The teacher gave a question card to the students comprising of analysis-based questions related to the topic and asked them to discuss the possible answers. Here, the teacher brought the attention of the students in front of the class and provided an opportunity to each group representative to present the answers by summarizing the responses of each member of the group. The other students were encouraged to pose essential questions before the group representative. Here, the teacher provided a question card to each group for discussion.

Question Card

Q1. What are the implications of the views of Rousseau on role of teacher?

Q2. Analyse the merits and drawbacks of free discipline prescribed by Rousseau with suitable example.

Q3. Analyse the educational contributions of Rousseau and represent in concept maps.

During the whole process, the students were encouraged to think aloud about the questions presented to them and asked them the following questions to themselves.

Q1. How are these questions related to the previous questions?

Q2. How will I use previous information to solve these questions?

Q3. Will I be able to connect my previous knowledge to this problem?

Q4. What kinds of difficulties am I facing to associate previous information?

Q5. What kinds of thoughts are running inside my mind concerned with this problem?

Q6. How can I solve these problems?

The students presented their answers in the group before the group representative, and the representative noted down the responses of each member and summarized the same. Finally, the representative presented the answers before others. The teacher encouraged other students to ask their queries to the representative. In this stage, both thinking-aloud and concept mapping strategies were used.

Evaluate:

In the fifth step i.e., Evaluate, the teacher and students both determined the extent to which the learning and understanding have taken place about

the topic, i.e., educational philosophy of Rousseau-II. Here, students were provided an opportunity to review and assess their learning in a summative form. Here, the students were encouraged to assess their understanding, abilities, skills, and behaviour related to the topic. The teacher gave due emphasis on reflection by following both formal and informal assessment procedures rather than traditional quizzes. The teacher gave due importance to self-assessment and writing assignments. The teacher preferred the self-assessment technique in this step, where the students got the opportunity to evaluate their own academic works and learning progress. Through self-assessment, the students got opportunity to identify the gap in their knowledge, track their own progress, set goals, and revise their works.

Activity-5

The teacher favoured some sorts of reflective questions related to the topic before the students and their responses were gathered orally. The reason behind the use of reflective questions was to encourage students for reflecting on their learning skills and generating relevant questions and ideas for propelling future learning experiences. In this stage, the teacher encouraged the students to ask questions about themselves related to their learning activities, processes, and behaviour.

Q1. Did I understand what I need to understand?

Q2. In which condition I learned the most?

Q3. Where did I feel difficulty in understanding the topic?

Q4. How did I learn the subject matter?

Q5. How my learning style is different from others?

Q6. Did I plan properly to adopt procedures for finding the solution to the problems?

Q7. Did I able to learn correctly about educational philosophy of Rousseau-III?

Q8. How did I learn the topic?

Q9. Do I keep in mind the way of my learning? How?

Q10. Am I satisfied with my learning style?

Q11. What is the lacuna in my learning?

Q12. How can I learn better?

The teacher gathered and analysed the responses of the students and measured the learning outcomes of the lesson. The teacher focused on students' abilities to formulate their own meaning and definitions about the topic. Here, the teacher used self-assessment technique.

Homework

At the end of the class, the teachers provided some home works related to the topic discussed before the class. The home works were given based on the students' learning and experience on the educational philosophy of Rousseau-III and also, they were instructed to gather information about the concept of learning, which was to be discussed in the next class. So, in this field, the teacher tried to prepare the students independently for the next class considering it as a technique of students' inspiration for further learning activities.

'The core points'- The students developed their deeper understanding regarding the educational philosophy of Rousseau and constructed new knowledge.

CHAPTER FOURTEEN

CONCEPT OF LEARNING

Lesson Plan-14

School: Higher Secondary School

Class: XII

Subject: Education

Topic: Concept of Learning

Duration: 1 hour

TLM Required: Education textbook, Laptop to show pictures, & Question

Approach: Constructivist with Metacognitive Interventions

Phases: Engage, Explore, Explain, Elaborate, & Evaluate

Aim and Objective: The objective of this class is to develop understanding among students about concept of learning.

Learning Outcomes: After the class, the students will be able to

- understand the concept of learning
- comprehend the definitions, nature and characteristics of learning
- demonstrate and evaluate their knowledge in terms of concept of learning

Engage:

In the first step of teaching i.e., Engage, the teacher favoured certain activities to capture and stimulate the attention, interest, thinking of the students. Here, the teacher tried to draw the child's curiosity towards learning and keep them mentally engaged in concepts, processes, or skills. So, keeping all these things in mind, the teacher performed the following

activity.

Activity-1

The teacher showed some photographs of some activities of children which they perform in their childhood and learn i.e., trying to touch fire, trying to be stand up, trying to run etc. Teacher: *Students, today, we shall make a discussion about concept of learning. What do you mean by learning? What are the nature and characteristics of learning?* The teacher allowed each student to answer individually. During this process, the students were instructed to ask the following questions to themselves independently and note down their reflections in their notebook.

Q1. What do I know about this?

Q2. What do I do not know about this?

Q3. What kind of question is this?

Q4. What do I need to know about these questions?

Q5. What should I do to get an idea to answer these questions?

Q6. What kind of goal should I set for this?

Q7. How can I solve the problem?

Q8. Which strategy will help to find a solution to the problem?

Here, the students were encouraged to think-aloud about the questions asked to them. During the whole process, the think-aloud strategy was followed, and the responses of each student were recorded.

Explore:

In the second step of teaching, the teacher provided scope to the students to get involved with the topic and build up their own understanding in groups depending upon the feasibility. In this phase, the students in groups got an opportunity to develop current concepts, processes, and skills as they explored the learning environment. Here, the teacher manipulated learning materials related to the topic and asked the students to go through the same thoroughly in their group. In this step, the students got time to think, plan, investigate, and organize the information collected or received by them. The role of the teacher was as a facilitator.

Activity-2

After few minutes, the teacher divided the whole class into some small groups by assigning 5-6 students in each group. During this, the teacher allowed each student of each group to present a solution to the problem. In this stage, each student was encouraged to ask the necessary questions to other students of their groups. So, each student presented solutions to the problem before the group representative and they arrived at the

consensus. After this, the group discussed their procedures to give solutions to the problem, where each member presented his/her procedures before others, and others listened to the presentation, analysed critically, and asked critical questions. At the end of the presentation, the students arrived at the consensus about the procedures of solving the problems. In this stage, the students were encouraged to ask the following questions to themselves individually.

Q1. How did I get my answer?

Q2. What will be other possible solutions to these problems?

Q3. Which strategy is the best to solve this problem?

Q4. How did I arrange the information for solving the problems?

Q5. What kinds of difficulties did you face to solve these problems?

Q6. How did I think about the procedures?

Q7. What are the limitations of this strategy?

During this stage, the students were encouraged to think aloud for finding possible solutions to the problem and work collaboratively. In this stage, the brainstorming method was encouraged.

Explain:

In the third step of teaching, the teacher provided the opportunity to the students for assimilation, where the students tried to connect their previous knowledge with the current learning for the conceptual clarity. Here, more focus was on students' attention on a specific part of engagement and exploration, which helped students to verbalize their conceptual understanding or demonstrating skills.

Activity-3

In this phase, the group representative presented the answers to the given problem before the group and showed a concept map for better visualisation and understanding. The group representatives got equal time to demonstrate their procedure of solving the problem, and the others actively listened to the presenters and posed essential questions to themselves.

Q1. How is this the solution to the problems?

Q2. Are there any other possible solutions?

Q3. Am I able to understand this solution?

Q4. What was running in my mind while listening to the solutions?

Q5. How is my procedure different from others?

During this phase, the teacher also got the opportunity to introduce the definition of the concepts, skills, process, and behaviour. Here, the

teacher encouraged the use of concept mapping strategy among students and assisted them to relate a concept with other sub-concepts in diagrams. The rationale behind the use of concept mapping strategy was to help the students in understanding relationship between concept and sub-concepts relating to the topic. Here the students worked in group to create concept maps related to the topic and showed to each other.

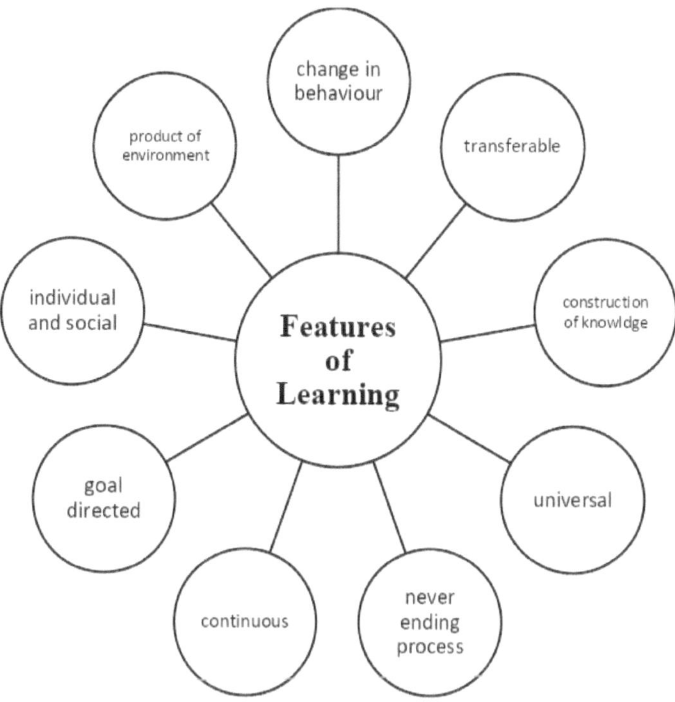

Figure-14: Features of learning

The teacher observed the whole process and provided the required assistance wherever required for a better understanding of the students. At the end of this phase, the teacher helped the group to arrive at the consensus of the problem.

Elaborate:

In the fourth step, the focus was given to students' conceptual understanding to allow them for practising different skills and behaviour. Here, the opportunity was provided to the students to apply or extend the previously learned concepts and experiences to the new situations, as

a result of which, the students developed better understanding, generated more information, and learned adequate skills. Here, the teacher helped the students to apply their learned knowledge and develop a deeper understanding of the subject matter.

Activity: 4

The teacher gave a question card to the students comprising of analysis-based questions related to the topic and asked them to discuss the possible answers. Here, the teacher brought the attention of the students in front of the class and provided an opportunity to each group representative to present the answers by summarizing the responses of each member of the group. The other students were encouraged to pose essential questions before the group representative. Here, the teacher provided a question card to each group for discussion.

Question Card

Q1. Learning is the modification of behaviour through experience. Elucidate.

Q2. How learning is both individual and social? Give your answers with suitable examples.

Q3. Analyse the concept of learning and find out the features of learning, and present in concept map?

During the whole process, the students were encouraged to think aloud about the questions presented to them and asked them the following questions to themselves.

Q1. How are these questions related to the previous questions?

Q2. How will I use previous information to solve these questions?

Q3. Will I be able to connect my previous knowledge to this problem?

Q4. What kinds of difficulties am I facing to associate previous information?

Q5. What kinds of thoughts are running inside my mind concerned with this problem?

Q6. How can I solve these problems?

The students presented their answers in the group before the group representative, and the representative noted down the responses of each member and summarized the same. Finally, the representative presented the answers before others. The teacher encouraged other students to ask their queries to the representative. In this stage, both thinking-aloud and concept mapping strategies were used.

Evaluate:

In the fifth step i.e., Evaluate, the teacher and students both determined the extent to which the learning and understanding have taken place about

the topic, i.e., concept of learning. Here, students were provided an opportunity to review and assess their learning in a summative form. Here, the students were encouraged to assess their understanding, abilities, skills, and behaviour related to the topic. The teacher gave due emphasis on reflection by following both formal and informal assessment procedures rather than traditional quizzes. The teacher gave due importance to self-assessment and writing assignments. The teacher preferred the self-assessment technique in this step, where the students got the opportunity to evaluate their own academic works and learning progress. Through self-assessment, the students got opportunity to identify the gap in their knowledge, track their own progress, set goals, and revise their works.

Activity-5

The teacher favoured some sorts of reflective questions related to the topic before the students and their responses were gathered orally. The reason behind the use of reflective questions was to encourage students for reflecting on their learning skills and generating relevant questions and ideas for propelling future learning experiences. In this stage, the teacher encouraged the students to ask questions about themselves related to their learning activities, processes, and behaviour.

Q1. Did I understand what I need to understand?

Q2. In which condition I learned the most?

Q3. Where did I feel difficulty in understanding the topic?

Q4. How did I learn the subject matter?

Q5. How my learning style is different from others?

Q6. Did I plan properly to adopt procedures for finding the solution to the problems?

Q7. Did I able to learn correctly about concept of learning?

Q8. How did I learn the topic?

Q9. Do I keep in mind the way of my learning? How?

Q10. Am I satisfied with my learning style?

Q11. What is the lacuna in my learning?

Q12. How can I learn better?

The teacher gathered and analysed the responses of the students and measured the learning outcomes of the lesson. The teacher focused on students' abilities to formulate their own meaning and definitions about the topic. Here, the teacher used self-assessment techniques through this phase.

Homework

At the end of the class, the teachers provided some home works related to the topic discussed before the class. The home works were given based on the students' learning and experience on the concept of learning and also, they were instructed to gather information about the factors affecting learning, which was to be discussed in the next class. So, in this field, the teacher tried to prepare the students independently for the next class considering it as a technique of students' inspiration for further learning activities.

'The core points'- The students developed their understanding regarding concept of learning and constructed new knowledge.

CHAPTER FIFTEEN

Factors affecting Learning

Lesson Plan-15

School: Higher Secondary School

Class: XII

Subject: Education

Topic: Factors affecting Learning

Duration: 1 hour

TLM Required: Education textbook, Laptop to show pictures, & Question

Approach: Constructivist with Metacognitive Interventions

Phases: Engage, Explore, Explain, Elaborate, & Evaluate

Aim and Objective: The objective of this class is to develop understanding among students about factors affecting learning.

Learning Outcomes: After the class, the students will be able to

- understand important factors affecting learning
- differentiate among different factors affecting learning
- demonstrate and evaluate their knowledge in terms of factors affecting learning

Engage:

In the first step of teaching i.e., Engage, the teacher favoured certain activities to capture and stimulate the attention, interest, thinking of the students. Here, the teacher tried to draw the child's curiosity towards learning and keep them mentally engaged in concepts, processes, or skills. So, keeping all these things in mind, the teacher performed the following

activity.

Activity-1

The teacher showed some photographs of some activities of learning of children in different places like school, home, playground etc. Teacher: *Students, today, we shall make a discussion about factors affecting learning. What are the important factors affecting learning?* The teacher allowed each student to answer individually. During this process, the students were instructed to ask the following questions to themselves independently and note down their reflections in their notebook.

Q1. What do I know about this?

Q2. What do I do not know about this?

Q3. What kind of question is this?

Q4. What do I need to know about these questions?

Q5. What should I do to get an idea to answer these questions?

Q6. What kind of goal should I set for this?

Q7. How can I solve the problem?

Q8. Which strategy will help to find a solution to the problem?

Here, the students were encouraged to think-aloud about the questions asked to them. During the whole process, the think-aloud strategy was followed, and the responses of each student were recorded.

Explore:

In the second step of teaching, the teacher provided scope to the students to get involved with the topic and build up their own understanding in groups depending upon the feasibility. In this phase, the students in groups got an opportunity to develop current concepts, processes, and skills as they explored the learning environment. Here, the teacher manipulated learning materials related to the topic and asked the students to go through the same thoroughly in their group. In this step, the students got time to think, plan, investigate, and organize the information collected or received by them. The role of the teacher was as a facilitator.

Activity-2

After few minutes, the teacher divided the whole class into some small groups by assigning 5-6 students in each group. During this, the teacher allowed each student of each group to present a solution to the problem. In this stage, each student was encouraged to ask the necessary questions to other students of their groups. So, each student presented solutions to the problem before the group representative and they arrived at the consensus. After this, the group discussed their procedures to give solutions to the problem, where each member presented his/her procedures before others, and others listened to the presentation, analysed critically, and asked critical questions. At the end of the presentation, the students arrived at the consensus about the procedures of solving the problems. In this stage, the students were encouraged to ask the following questions to themselves individually.

Q1. How did I get my answer?

Q2. What will be other possible solutions to these problems?

Q3. Which strategy is the best to solve this problem?

Q4. How did I arrange the information for solving the problems?

Q5. What kinds of difficulties did you face to solve these problems?

Q6. How did I think about the procedures?

Q7. What are the limitations of this strategy?

During this stage, the students were encouraged to think aloud for finding possible solutions to the problem and work collaboratively. In this stage, the brainstorming method was encouraged.

Explain:

In the third step of teaching, the teacher provided the opportunity to the students for assimilation, where the students tried to connect their previous knowledge with the current learning for the conceptual clarity. Here, more focus was on students' attention on a specific part of engagement and exploration, which helped students to verbalize their conceptual understanding or demonstrating skills.

Activity-3

In this phase, the group representative presented the answers to the given problem before the group and showed a concept map for better visualisation and understanding. The group representatives got equal time to demonstrate their procedure of solving the problem, and the others actively listened to the presenters and posed essential questions to themselves.

Q1. How is this the solution to the problems?

Q2. Are there any other possible solutions?

Q3. Am I able to understand this solution?

Q4. What was running in my mind while listening to the solutions?

Q5. How is my procedure different from others?

During this phase, the teacher also got the opportunity to introduce the definition of the concepts, skills, process, and behaviour. Here, the teacher encouraged the use of concept mapping strategy among students and assisted them to relate a concept with other sub-concepts in diagrams. The rationale behind the use of concept mapping strategy was to help the students in understanding relationship between concept and sub-concepts relating to the topic. Here the students worked in group to create concept maps related to the topic and showed to each other.

Figure-15: Factors affecting learning

The teacher observed the whole process and provided the required assistance wherever required for a better understanding of the students. At the end of this phase, the teacher helped the group to arrive at the consensus of the problem.

Elaborate:

In the fourth step, the focus was given to students' conceptual understanding to allow them for practising different skills and behaviour. Here, the opportunity was provided to the students to apply or extend the previously learned concepts and experiences to the new situations, as

a result of which, the students developed better understanding, generated more information, and learned adequate skills. Here, the teacher helped the students to apply their learned knowledge and develop a deeper understanding of the subject matter.

Activity: 4

The teacher gave a question card to the students comprising of analysis-based questions related to the topic and asked them to discuss the possible answers. Here, the teacher brought the attention of the students in front of the class and provided an opportunity to each group representative to present the answers by summarizing the responses of each member of the group. The other students were encouraged to pose essential questions before the group representative. Here, the teacher provided a question card to each group for discussion.

Question Card

Q1. Learning is the influenced by both internal and external factors. Discuss with suitable examples.

Q2. What are the factors affecting learning in this present era? Give suitable examples.

Q3. Analyse the factors affecting learning in educational context, and present your answer in concept maps.

During the whole process, the students were encouraged to think aloud about the questions presented to them and asked them the following questions to themselves.

Q1. How are these questions related to the previous questions?

Q2. How will I use previous information to solve these questions?

Q3. Will I be able to connect my previous knowledge to this problem?

Q4. What kinds of difficulties am I facing to associate previous information?

Q5. What kinds of thoughts are running inside my mind concerned with this problem?

Q6. How can I solve these problems?

The students presented their answers in the group before the group representative, and the representative noted down the responses of each member and summarized the same. Finally, the representative presented the answers before others. The teacher encouraged other students to ask their queries to the representative. In this stage, both thinking-aloud and concept mapping strategies were used.

Evaluate:

In the fifth step i.e., Evaluate, the teacher and students both determined the extent to which the learning and understanding have taken place about the topic, i.e., factors affecting learning. Here, students were provided an opportunity to review and assess their learning in a summative form. Here, the students were encouraged to assess their understanding, abilities, skills, and behaviour related to the topic. The teacher gave due emphasis on reflection by following both formal and informal assessment procedures rather than traditional quizzes. The teacher gave due importance to self-assessment and writing assignments. The teacher preferred the self-assessment technique in this step, where the students got the opportunity to evaluate their own academic works and learning progress. Through self-assessment, the students got opportunity to identify the gap in their knowledge, track their own progress, set goals, and revise their works.

Activity-5

The teacher favoured some sorts of reflective questions related to the topic before the students and their responses were gathered orally. The reason behind the use of reflective questions was to encourage students for reflecting on their learning skills and generating relevant questions and ideas for propelling future learning experiences. In this stage, the teacher encouraged the students to ask questions about themselves related to their learning activities, processes, and behaviour.

Q1. Did I understand what I need to understand?

Q2. In which condition I learned the most?

Q3. Where did I feel difficulty in understanding the topic?

Q4. How did I learn the subject matter?

Q5. How my learning style is different from others?

Q6. Did I plan properly to adopt procedures for finding the solution to the problems?

Q7. Did I able to learn correctly about factors affecting learning?

Q8. How did I learn the topic?

Q9. Do I keep in mind the way of my learning? How?

Q10. Am I satisfied with my learning style?

Q11. What is the lacuna in my learning?

Q12. How can I learn better?

The teacher gathered and analysed the responses of the students and measured the learning outcomes of the lesson. The teacher focused on students' abilities to formulate their own meaning and definitions about the topic. Here, the teacher used self-assessment techniques through this phase.

Homework

At the end of the class, the teachers provided some home works related to the topic discussed before the class. The home works were given based on the students' learning and experience on the factors affecting learning and also, they were instructed to gather information about theories of learning, which was to be discussed in the next class. So, in this field, the teacher tried to prepare the students independently for the next class considering it as a technique of students' inspiration for further learning activities.

'The core points'- The students developed their understanding regarding the factors affecting learning and constructed new knowledge.

CHAPTER SIXTEEN

TRIAL AND ERROR THEORY OF LEARNING

Lesson Plan-16

School: Higher Secondary School

Class: XII

Subject: Education

Topic: Trial and Error Theory of Learning

Duration: 1 hour

TLM Required: Education textbook, Laptop to show pictures, & Question

Approach: Constructivist with Metacognitive Interventions

Phases: Engage, Explore, Explain, Elaborate, & Evaluate

Aim and Objective: The objective of this class is to develop understanding among students about trial and error theory of learning.

Learning Outcomes: After the class, the students will be able to

- understand the concept of trial and error theory of learning
- comprehend the experiment of trial and error theory of learning
- demonstrate and evaluate their knowledge in terms of trail and error theory of learning

Engage:

In the first step of teaching i.e., Engage, the teacher favoured certain activities to capture and stimulate the attention, interest, thinking of the students. Here, the teacher tried to draw the child's curiosity towards learning and keep them mentally engaged in concepts, processes, or skills. So, keeping all these things in mind, the teacher performed the following

activity.

Activity-1

The teacher presented some examples of practices that the children usually do in their childhood, learn the same practice and also do the same in their adolescence. Teacher: *Students, today, we shall make a discussion about trial and error theory of learning. What is trial and error theory of learning? Discuss Thorndike's experiment on cat.* The teacher allowed each student to answer individually. During this process, the students were instructed to ask the following questions to themselves independently and note down their reflections in their notebook.

Q1. What do I know about this?

Q2. What do I do not know about this?

Q3. What kind of question is this?

Q4. What do I need to know about these questions?

Q5. What should I do to get an idea to answer these questions?

Q6. What kind of goal should I set for this?

Q7. How can I solve the problem?

Q8. Which strategy will help to find a solution to the problem?

Here, the students were encouraged to think-aloud about the questions asked to them. During the whole process, the think-aloud strategy was followed, and the responses of each student were recorded.

Explore:

In the second step of teaching, the teacher provided scope to the students to get involved with the topic and build up their own understanding in groups depending upon the feasibility. In this phase, the students in groups got an opportunity to develop current concepts, processes, and skills as they explored the learning environment. Here, the teacher manipulated learning materials related to the topic and asked the students to go through the same thoroughly in their group. In this step, the students got time to think, plan, investigate, and organize the information collected or received by them. The role of the teacher was as a facilitator.

Activity-2

After few minutes, the teacher divided the whole class into some small groups by assigning 5-6 students in each group. During this, the teacher allowed each student of each group to present a solution to the problem. In this stage, each student was encouraged to ask the necessary questions to other students of their groups. So, each student presented solutions to the problem before the group representative and they arrived at the

consensus. After this, the group discussed their procedures to give solutions to the problem, where each member presented his/her procedures before others, and others listened to the presentation, analysed critically, and asked critical questions. At the end of the presentation, the students arrived at the consensus about the procedures of solving the problems. In this stage, the students were encouraged to ask the following questions to themselves individually.

Q1. How did I get my answer?

Q2. What will be other possible solutions to these problems?

Q3. Which strategy is the best to solve this problem?

Q4. How did I arrange the information for solving the problems?

Q5. What kinds of difficulties did you face to solve these problems?

Q6. How did I think about the procedures?

Q7. What are the limitations of this strategy?

During this stage, the students were encouraged to think aloud for finding possible solutions to the problem and work collaboratively. In this stage, the brainstorming method was encouraged.

Explain:

In the third step of teaching, the teacher provided the opportunity to the students for assimilation, where the students tried to connect their previous knowledge with the current learning for the conceptual clarity. Here, more focus was on students' attention on a specific part of engagement and exploration, which helped students to verbalize their conceptual understanding or demonstrating skills.

Activity-3

In this phase, the group representative presented the answers to the given problem before the group and showed a concept map for better visualisation and understanding. The group representatives got equal time to demonstrate their procedure of solving the problem, and the others actively listened to the presenters and posed essential questions to themselves.

Q1. How is this the solution to the problems?

Q2. Are there any other possible solutions?

Q3. Am I able to understand this solution?

Q4. What was running in my mind while listening to the solutions?

Q5. How is my procedure different from others?

During this phase, the teacher also got the opportunity to introduce the definition of the concepts, skills, process, and behaviour. Here, the

teacher encouraged the use of concept mapping strategy among students and assisted them to relate a concept with other sub-concepts in diagrams. The rationale behind the use of concept mapping strategy was to help the students in understanding relationship between concept and sub-concepts relating to the topic. Here the students worked in group to create concept maps related to the topic and showed to each other.

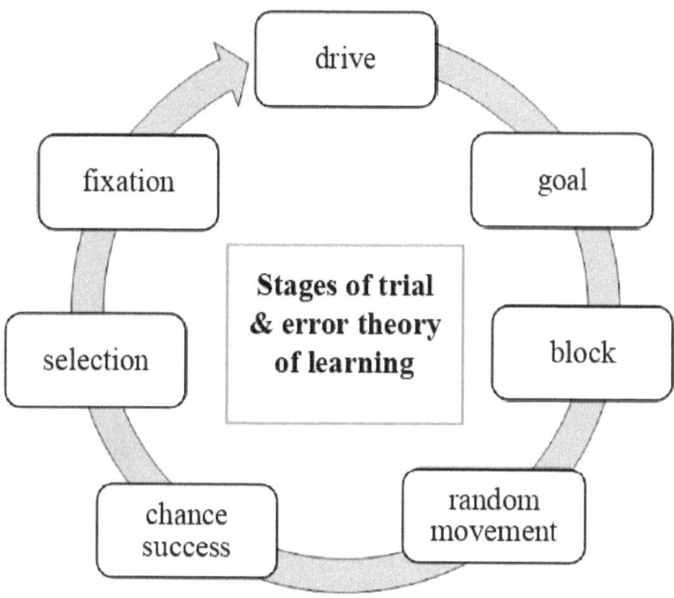

Figure-16: Stages of trial and error theory of learning

The teacher observed the whole process and provided the required assistance wherever required for a better understanding of the students. At the end of this phase, the teacher helped the group to arrive at the consensus of the problem.

Elaborate:

In the fourth step, the focus was given to students' conceptual understanding to allow them for practising different skills and behaviour. Here, the opportunity was provided to the students to apply or extend the previously learned concepts and experiences to the new situations, as a result of which, the students developed better understanding, generated more information, and learned adequate skills. Here, the teacher helped the students to apply their learned knowledge and develop a deeper understanding of the subject matter.

Activity: 4

The teacher gave a question card to the students comprising of analysis-based questions related to the topic and asked them to discuss the possible answers. Here, the teacher brought the attention of the students in front of the class and provided an opportunity to each group representative to present the answers by summarizing the responses of each member of the group. The other students were encouraged to pose essential questions before the group representative. Here, the teacher provided a question card to each group for discussion.

Question Card

Q1. What do you mean by trial and error theory of learning? Define it with your own words by citing an example.

Q2. Analyse the systematic stage that the cat followed in trial and error theory of learning, and present your answer in concept map.

Q3. Discuss similar experiment of your real-life situation as presented in trial and error theory of learning.

During the whole process, the students were encouraged to think aloud about the questions presented to them and asked them the following questions to themselves.

Q1. How are these questions related to the previous questions?

Q2. How will I use previous information to solve these questions?

Q3. Will I be able to connect my previous knowledge to this problem?

Q4. What kinds of difficulties am I facing to associate previous information?

Q5. What kinds of thoughts are running inside my mind concerned with this problem?

Q6. How can I solve these problems?

The students presented their answers in the group before the group representative, and the representative noted down the responses of each member and summarized the same. Finally, the representative presented the answers before others. The teacher encouraged other students to ask their queries to the representative. In this stage, both thinking-aloud and concept mapping strategies were used.

Evaluate:

In the fifth step i.e., Evaluate, the teacher and students both determined the extent to which the learning and understanding have taken place about

the topic, i.e., trial and error theory of learning. Here, students were provided an opportunity to review and assess their learning in a summative form. Here, the students were encouraged to assess their understanding, abilities, skills, and behaviour related to the topic. The teacher gave due emphasis on reflection by following both formal and informal assessment procedures rather than traditional quizzes. The teacher gave due importance to self-assessment and writing assignments. The teacher preferred the self-assessment technique in this step, where the students got the opportunity to evaluate their own academic works and learning progress. Through self-assessment, the students got opportunity to identify the gap in their knowledge, track their own progress, set goals, and revise their works.

Activity-5

The teacher favoured some sorts of reflective questions related to the topic before the students and their responses were gathered orally. The reason behind the use of reflective questions was to encourage students for reflecting on their learning skills and generating relevant questions and ideas for propelling future learning experiences. In this stage, the teacher encouraged the students to ask questions about themselves related to their learning activities, processes, and behaviour.

Q1. Did I understand what I need to understand?

Q2. In which condition I learned the most?

Q3. Where did I feel difficulty in understanding the topic?

Q4. How did I learn the subject matter?

Q5. How my learning style is different from others?

Q6. Did I plan properly to adopt procedures for finding the solution to the problems?

Q7. Did I able to learn correctly about trial and error theory of learning?

Q8. How did I learn the topic?

Q9. Do I keep in mind the way of my learning? How?

Q10. Am I satisfied with my learning style?

Q11. What is the lacuna in my learning?

Q12. How can I learn better?

The teacher gathered and analysed the responses of the students and measured the learning outcomes of the lesson. The teacher focused on students' abilities to formulate their own meaning and definitions about the topic. Here, the teacher used self-assessment techniques through this phase.

Homework

At the end of the class, the teachers provided some home works related to the topic discussed before the class. The home works were given based on the students' learning and experience on the trial and error theory of learning and also, they were instructed to gather information about the laws of learning as prescribed by Thorndike, which was to be discussed in the next class. So, in this field, the teacher tried to prepare the students independently for the next class considering it as a technique of students' inspiration for further learning activities.

'The core points'- The students developed their understanding regarding trial and error theory of learning and constructed new knowledge.

LAWS OF LEARNING

Lesson Plan-17

School: Higher Secondary School

Class: XII

Subject: Education

Topic: Laws of Learning

Duration: 1 hour

TLM Required: Education textbook, Laptop to show pictures, & Question

Approach: Constructivist with Metacognitive Interventions

Phases: Engage, Explore, Explain, Elaborate, & Evaluate

Aim and Objective: The objective of this class is to develop understanding among students about laws of learning.

Learning Outcomes: After the class, the students will be able to

- understand the laws of learning
- compare among laws of exercise, readiness and effect
- demonstrate their knowledge in terms of laws of learning

Engage:

In the first step of teaching i.e., Engage, the teacher favoured certain activities to capture and stimulate the attention, interest, thinking of the students. Here, the teacher tried to draw the child's curiosity towards learning and keep them mentally engaged in concepts, processes, or skills. So, keeping all these things in mind, the teacher performed the following activity.

Activity-1

The teacher showed some photographs of childing practising some activities like cycling, climbing tree etc., and asked the students to share their ideas related to the pictures. Teacher: *Students, today, we shall make a discussion about the laws of learning. What do you mean by laws of learning? What are the laws of learning given by Thorndike?* The teacher allowed each student to answer individually. During this process, the students were instructed to ask the following questions to themselves independently and note down their reflections in their notebook.

Q1. What do I know about this?

Q2. What do I do not know about this?

Q3. What kind of question is this?

Q4. What do I need to know about these questions?

Q5. What should I do to get an idea to answer these questions?

Q6. What kind of goal should I set for this?

Q7. How can I solve the problem?

Q8. Which strategy will help to find a solution to the problem?

Here, the students were encouraged to think-aloud about the questions asked to them. During the whole process, the think-aloud strategy was followed, and the responses of each student were recorded.

Explore:

In the second step of teaching, the teacher provided scope to the students to get involved with the topic and build up their own understanding in groups depending upon the feasibility. In this phase, the students in groups got an opportunity to develop current concepts, processes, and skills as they explored the learning environment. Here, the teacher manipulated learning materials related to the topic and asked the students to go through the same thoroughly in their group. In this step, the students got time to think, plan, investigate, and organize the information collected or received by them. The role of the teacher was as a facilitator.

Activity-2

After few minutes, the teacher divided the whole class into some small groups by assigning 5-6 students in each group. During this, the teacher allowed each student of each group to present a solution to the problem. In this stage, each student was encouraged to ask the necessary questions to other students of their groups. So, each student presented solutions to the problem before the group representative and they arrived at the consensus. After this, the group discussed their procedures to give solutions to the problem, where each member presented his/her procedures before others, and others listened to the presentation, analysed critically, and asked critical questions. At the end of the presentation, the students arrived at the consensus about the procedures of solving the problems. In this stage, the students were encouraged to ask the following questions to themselves individually.

Q1. How did I get my answer?

Q2. What will be other possible solutions to these problems?

Q3. Which strategy is the best to solve this problem?

Q4. How did I arrange the information for solving the problems?

Q5. What kinds of difficulties did you face to solve these problems?

Q6. How did I think about the procedures?

Q7. What are the limitations of this strategy?

During this stage, the students were encouraged to think aloud for finding possible solutions to the problem and work collaboratively. In this stage, the brainstorming method was encouraged.

Explain:

In the third step of teaching, the teacher provided the opportunity to the students for assimilation, where the students tried to connect their previous knowledge with the current learning for the conceptual clarity. Here, more focus was on students' attention on a specific part of engagement and exploration, which helped students to verbalize their conceptual understanding or demonstrating skills.

Activity-3

In this phase, the group representative presented the answers to the given problem before the group and showed a concept map for better visualisation and understanding. The group representatives got equal time to demonstrate their procedure of solving the problem, and the others actively listened to the presenters and posed essential questions to themselves.

Q1. How is this the solution to the problems?

Q2. Are there any other possible solutions?

Q3. Am I able to understand this solution?

Q4. What was running in my mind while listening to the solutions?

Q5. How is my procedure different from others?

During this phase, the teacher also got the opportunity to introduce the definition of the concepts, skills, process, and behaviour. Here, the teacher encouraged the use of concept mapping strategy among students and assisted them to relate a concept with other sub-concepts in diagrams.

The rationale behind the use of concept mapping strategy was to help the students in understanding relationship between concept and sub-concepts relating to the topic. Here the students worked in group to create concept maps related to the topic and showed to each other.

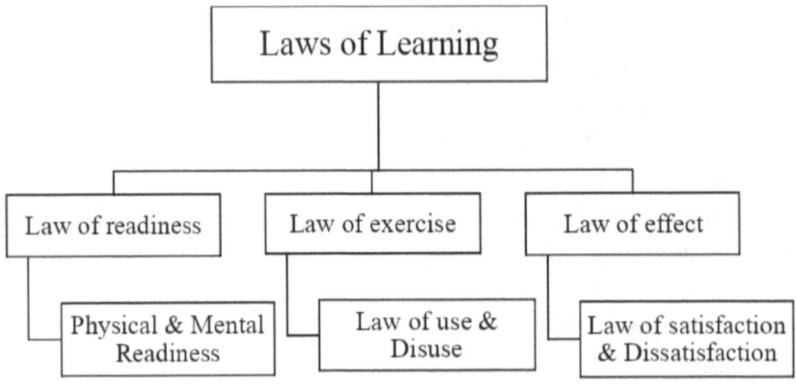

Figure-17: Laws of learning

The teacher observed the whole process and provided the required assistance wherever required for a better understanding of the students. At the end of this phase, the teacher helped the group to arrive at the consensus of the problem.

Elaborate:

In the fourth step, the focus was given to students' conceptual understanding to allow them for practising different skills and behaviour. Here, the opportunity was provided to the students to apply or extend the previously learned concepts and experiences to the new situations, as a result of which, the students developed better understanding, generated more information, and learned adequate skills. Here, the teacher helped the students to apply their learned knowledge and develop a deeper understanding of the subject matter.

Activity: 4

The teacher gave a question card to the students comprising of analysis-based questions related to the topic and asked them to discuss the possible answers. Here, the teacher brought the attention of the students in front of the class and provided an opportunity to each group representative to present the answers by summarizing the responses of each member of the group. The other students were encouraged to pose essential questions before the group representative. Here, the teacher provided a question card to each group for discussion.

Question Card

Q1. Give suitable examples of laws of learning relating to present scenario.

Q2. Make a comparative analysis of the three laws of learning and present in diagrams.

Q3. Analyse the implications of these laws of learning in classroom context at present?

During the whole process, the students were encouraged to think aloud about the questions presented to them and asked them the following questions to themselves.

Q1. How are these questions related to the previous questions?

Q2. How will I use previous information to solve these questions?

Q3. Will I be able to connect my previous knowledge to this problem?

Q4. What kinds of difficulties am I facing to associate previous information?

Q5. What kinds of thoughts are running inside my mind concerned with this problem?

Q6. How can I solve these problems?

The students presented their answers in the group before the group representative, and the representative noted down the responses of each member and summarized the same. Finally, the representative presented the answers before others. The teacher encouraged other students to ask their queries to the representative. In this stage, both thinking-aloud and concept mapping strategies were used.

Evaluate:

In the fifth step i.e., Evaluate, the teacher and students both determined the extent to which the learning and understanding have taken place about the topic, i.e., laws of learning. Here, students were provided an opportunity to review and assess their learning in a summative form. Here, the students were encouraged to assess their understanding, abilities, skills, and behaviour related to the topic. The teacher gave due emphasis on reflection by following both formal and informal assessment procedures rather than traditional quizzes. The teacher gave due importance to self-assessment and writing assignments. The teacher preferred the self-assessment technique in this step, where the students got the opportunity to evaluate their own academic works and learning progress. Through self-assessment, the students got opportunity to identify the gap in their knowledge, track their own progress, set goals, and revise their works.

Activity-5

The teacher favoured some sorts of reflective questions related to the topic before the students and their responses were gathered orally. The reason behind the use of reflective questions was to encourage students for reflecting on their learning skills and generating relevant questions and ideas for propelling future learning experiences. In this stage, the teacher encouraged the students to ask questions about themselves related to their learning activities, processes, and behaviour.

Q1. Did I understand what I need to understand?

Q2. In which condition I learned the most?

Q3. Where did I feel difficulty in understanding the topic?

Q4. How did I learn the subject matter?

Q5. How my learning style is different from others?

Q6. Did I plan properly to adopt procedures for finding the solution to the problems?

Q7. Did I able to learn correctly about laws of learning?

Q8. How did I learn the topic?

Q9. Do I keep in mind the way of my learning? How?

Q10. Am I satisfied with my learning style?

Q11. What is the lacuna in my learning?

Q12. How can I learn better?

The teacher gathered and analysed the responses of the students and measured the learning outcomes of the lesson. The teacher focused on students' abilities to formulate their own meaning and definitions about the topic. Here, the teacher used self-assessment techniques through this phase.

Homework

At the end of the class, the teachers provided some home works related to the topic discussed before the class. The home works were given based on the students' learning and experience on the laws of learning. So, in this field, the teacher tried to prepare the students independently for the next class considering it as a technique of students' inspiration for further learning activities.

'The core points'- The students developed their understanding regarding the laws of learning and constructed new knowledge.

Bibliography

Alshammari, M. K. (2015). Effective brainstorming in teaching social studies for elementary school. *American International Journal of Contemporary Research, 5*(2), 60-65.

Alshammari, M. K. (2015). The effect of using metacognitive strategies for achievement and the trend towards social studies for intermediate school students in Saudi Arabia. *International Journal of Education, 3*(7), 47-54.

Baddareen, G. A., Ghaith, S., & Akour, M. (2015). Self-efficacy, achievement goals, and metacognition as predicator of academic motivation. *Procedia-Social and Behavioural Sciences, 191*, 2068-2073.

Bandura, A. (1982a). Self-efficacy: Towards a unifying theory of behavioural change *Psychological Review, 84*, 191-215.

Bandura, A. (1982b). Self-efficacy mechanism in human agency. *American Psychologist, 37*, 122-147. http://dx.doi.org/10.1037/0003-006X.37.2.1.122

Bandura, A. (1983). Self-efficacy determinants of anticipated fears and calamities. *Journal of Personality and Social Psychology, 45*, 464-469.

Bandura, A. (1986). *Social foundation of thought and action: A social cognitive theory.* Englewood Cliffs, NJ: Prentice Hall.

Brown, A L. (1987). Metacognition, executive control, self-regulation, and other more mysterious mechanisms. In F. Weinert & R. Kluwe (Eds.), *Metacognition, motivation and understanding* (pp. 65–116). Hillsdale, NJ: Erlbaum.

Bybee, R (1993). *Instructional model for science education in developing biological literacy.* Colorado: Springs, CO.

Cikrikci, O., & Odaci, H. (2013). Investigating science high school students' metacognitive awareness and self-efficacy perceptions with respect to some individual and academic variables. *International Journal of Human Science, 10*(2), 246-259.

Cross, D. R. & Paris, S. G. (1988). Developmental and instructional analyses of children's metacognition and reading comprehension. *Journal of Educational Psychology, 80*(2), 131-142.

Flavell, J. H. (1963). *The developmental psychology of Jean Piaget.* New York: D, Van Nostrand.

Flavell, J. H. (1979). Metacognition and cognitive monitoring: A new area of cognitive-developmental inquiry. *American Psychologist, 34*(10), 906-911. http://doi.dx.10.1037/0003-066X.34.10.906.

Flavell, J. H. (1981). Cognitive monitoring. In W.P. Dickson (Ed.), *Children oral communication.* New York. Academic Press, pp. 35-60.

Flavell, J. H. (1985). *Cognitive development* (2nd Ed.). Englewood Cliffs, New York: Prentice Hall Inc.

Kuhn, D. (1999). A developmental model of critical thinking. *Educational Researchers, 28*(1), 16-26.

Kuhn, D., & Dean, D. (2004). A bridge between cognitive psychology and educational practice. *Theory into Practice, 43*(4), 268-273.

Miller, P. H. (1985). Metacognition and attention. In Forrest-Pressley, G. L. McKinnon, E. G., and Waller, T. G. (Eds.), *Metacognition, Cognition, and Human Performance* (pp.181-21). New York: Academic Press.

Mukhopadhyay, M. (2001). Secondary education: The challenge ahead. In Mukhopadhyay, M., & Narula, M. (Eds.), *Secondary education: The challenges ahead.* New Delhi: NIEPA.

Novak, J. D. (1990). Concept mapping: A useful tool for science education. *Journal of Research in Science Teaching, 27*(10), 937-949.

Schraw, G. & Moshman, D. (1995). Metacognitive theories. *Educational Psychology Review, 7*(4), 351-371.

Schunk, D. H. (2008). *Learning theories: An educational perspective.* Upper Saddler River, NJ.

Willing, K. (1990). *Teaching how to learn.* Sydney, Australia: National Centre for English Language Teaching and Research.

Zan, R. (2000). A metacognitive intervention in Mathematics at the university level. *International Journal of Mathematical Education in Science and Technology, 31*, 143-150.

Zimmerman, B. J. (2002). Becoming a self-regulated learner: An overview. *Theory into Practices, 41*(2), 64-70.

Zimmerman, B. J., & Martinez-Pons, M. (1990). Student differences in self-regulated learning: Relating grades, sex, and giftedness to self-efficacy and strategy use. *Journal of Educational Psychology, 82*(1), 51-59.

Thank
you
so
much!